I0091622

The Hummingbird Way is an energetic and thought-provoking guide to self-development. Gerek champions and inspires readers to do the internal work necessary to create a life with intention and integrity. For those wanting to shift their energy to a lofty state—this book flies high!

—Bruce D Schneider, Ph.D., M.C.C., founder of The Institute for Professional Excellence in Coaching (iPEC) and author of *Energy Leadership: Transforming Your Workplace and Your Life from the Core* and *Relax, You're Already Perfect*

The Hummingbird Way offers timeless tools for being your best. Gerek gently guides the reader toward greater self-awareness through reflection and action. Like a wise best friend, Gerek offers the way toward greater self-acceptance and greater peace with life as it is, while inspiring the reader to envision and achieve an extraordinary life.

—Kathy McDonald, MBA, Author of *Creating Your Life Collage: Strategies for Solving the Work/Life Dilemma*

A rich step-by-step guide to creating the kind of mind-set that becomes a life-long springboard for attaining success, and happiness. Gerek's brilliant combination of story and strategy make **The Hummingbird Way** a book to repeatedly reach for to achieve the next big goal or overcome any new challenge.
—Krystina Feucht, Director of Marketing Life Force International, Certified Professional Coach, Cofounder, Bookstrap Book Club

The Hummingbird Way is truly a guidebook for living a full and happy life. Sherri Gerek beautifully articulates how to reframe conversations and better understand the people you work with, live with and love the most. If you want to transform relationships with others—and most importantly, with yourself—you need to read this book.
—Jules Taggart, www.ampandpivot.com, Marketing Strategist, Blogger, Entrepreneur, Cofounder, Bootstrap Book Club

Sherri Gerek applies entertaining observations in nature to engaging life experiences allowing readers to reach heightened awareness, and soar further by internalizing the books easily relatable lessons. **The Hummingbird Way** was born of a grateful heart, and will forever be my resource—a shining reminder of who I really am, and how I want to show up in my life.
—Dawn Jackson, Director of Sales, The Lodge at Whitefish Lake

The Hummingbird Way

The Hummingbird Way

Putting Hover, Zip, and Zoom to Work in Your Life!

Sherri Lynea Gerek

Let's Strut Your Stuff

Copyright © 2014 by Sherri Lynea Gerek

All rights reserved. No part of this publication may be reproduced, stored in a retrieval system, or transmitted in any form or by any means, electronic, mechanical, photocopying, recording, or otherwise, without the prior written permission of the copyright holder, except brief quotations used in a review.

Printed in the United States of America.
Book design by Meadowlark Publishing Services.
Cover image: janedoedynamite/
Hummingbird hair series/Getty images.
Photo on page xx by Samuel Stockton White V
Hummingbirds and vine illustration by Oksanika/Shutterstock
Hummingbird silhouettes by Spyder/Shutterstock
Photos on pages 201, 202, and 207 by Sherri Gerek

ISBN 978-0-578-13605-9

Published 2014 by Let's Strut Your Stuff
www.letsstrutyourstuff.com

For the Love of all that is,
and Reverence for Life
I am dedicating this book to you,
dear reader.

Contents

Contents

Acknowledgments

*T*o my clients, and workshop attendees who have dared to open to the experience of collaborative work, I salute you. It is my honor to walk beside you, and bear witness to your remarkable journeys.*

With grateful acknowledgment I wish to thank the Institute for Professional Excellence in Coaching (iPEC), and founder Bruce D Schneider, for permission to further adapt concepts and tools from the iPEC coach training program. The lessons of Core Energy Coaching and Energy Leadership help create a tremendous platform for building solid personal and professional success.

Additionally, I want to recognize the iPEC coaches, instructors, and professionals I have come to know for their synergistic approach to work and life. An enthusiastic high five to your Level 6 Energy Liz Fisch, D. Luke Iorio, Janet O'Neil, and Francine Carter, I thank you all for the positivity. You walk your talk *beautifully.*

A hip-check, a broad smile, and a hearty *Right On*! to my coaching circle of friends, Kathy McDonald, Krystina Feucht, Sharon Madrid, Jenifer Johnson, Sally Falb, Susanne Walker, Barbara Blair, Tina Robbins, Valerie Freilich, Emelie D'Anna, and Tanya Ragbeer. Thank you all for the tireless inspiration, thoughtful insight, and whacky good humor.

To my editor, Sheridan McCarthy, I send *a knowing nod* and my heartfelt appreciation for her warm, and witty, *genius* ways.

Thank you Audrey Botha for the inspiring cover image of the

*Special note:
Names and identifying characteristics have been omitted for clients depicted in the book to protect their privacy. In some instances, clients are a composite of more than one individual.

Girl with Hummingbird Hair. Your work seemed destined to become my book cover. www.audreybotha.com

To my friends, and colleagues—thanks for the camaraderie, laughter, heart to heart conversations, and goodwill every step of the way. Hugs to you Tracy Ann, Tonya, Jennifer, Carrie, Judy, Dawnsie, Alicia, Dee Ann, Janey, and Kayme,

To my Mamala who lives life in a shining-lift-others-up kind of way every day, you never cease to amaze me, Linda Thomson. You taught me to be kind, to follow my heart, and to live with integrity. I am so fortunate to be your daughter!

To Teresa "Lilly" White, and Shelley "Shelby" Thomson, my sisters, and to all of my family who hold a sacred space in my heart, although the miles between us may at times be great, I carry your spirits close to me always.

To the Love of my Life, Larry, who seemingly waved his magic wand over me, and with it cast the most magnificent spell, I thank you for this fairy tale come true. I love you more, Larry G.

A portion of the proceeds from sales of *The Hummingbird Way* will benefit these organizations which serve the general well-being, education, and self-development of women:

Montana Woman Foundation   montanawoman.com

Safe Harbor   safeharbormt.org

Susan G. Komen for the Cure   ww5.komen.org

Disclaimers

With respect to ornithologists everywhere, I declare myself a novice lifelong learner whose interest in the hummingbirds is to broaden the reader's understanding, and perhaps dispel a few myths along the way. As a result of personal observation, and online research I aspire to share some of what I have found interesting about the hummingbirds characteristics, habits, and behaviors.

While I do not profess to be a hummingbird expert, I endeavor to use my personal observations and findings as a tool to draw analogies with hopes you, the reader, will see nature through a new lens—as a reflection of your own phenomenal spirit.

If you would like to learn more about hummingbirds the following websites are a good source of information*:

National Audubon Society	www.audubon.org
Smithsonian's National Zoo	www.nationalzoo.si.edu
National Park Service	www.nps.gov/cham/nature science/hbirds.htm
The Hummingbird Society	www.hummingbirdsociety.org
World of Hummingbirds.com	www.worldofhummingbirds.com
The Annenberg Foundation— Journey North	www.learner.org/jnorth/search/ Hummer

*All Web addresses and URLs were valid at the time of printing.

Introduction

I am grateful for the opportunity to live in one of the most breathtakingly beautiful areas of the country: the Flathead Valley of northwestern Montana, just a stone's throw away from Glacier National Park. I feel fortunate that my husband, Larry, and I are stewards of this remarkable land we share with some of the very best nature that life has to offer.

We regularly witness herds of whitetail deer grazing in our meadow, flocks of geese assembling on the river below our home, bald eagles perched in the pines off our west deck, and an abundance of wildlife sightings that ensure we keep binoculars and a spotting scope at the ready at all times.

Over the years we have had numerous amazing—and often entertaining—encounters with a host of animals on our property: bobcats, wolf, grizzly bear, wolverine, cougar, raccoon, skunk, fox, and coyotes. An albino black bear even came up on the deck near our bedroom late one night!

There I was, shaking the cobwebs out of my head at 3 a.m. while our trusty Labrador barked incessantly to alert us to the bear's presence. I thought I might have been transported to Alaska during my sleep, for what I saw when I looked out on the deck was quite clearly a polar bear. Upon hearing the low guttural growls coming from our mild-mannered dog, the blonde bear lumbered clumsily down the stairs from the deck to the path, on through the woods below, and out of our lives. Such a gorgeous creature, the albino black bear: truly a vision to behold.

Yes, wildlife is abundant here. In addition to the many four-legged creatures that live in this natural paradise, we also share our space with many feathered friends. Frequent visitors include the pileated woodpeckers, great horned owls, golden eagles, red-tailed hawks, bluebirds, robins, magpies, swans, geese, northern flickers, and yes . . . hummingbirds.

Oh, those hummingbirds, appearing to visibly express an inner jubilant, joyous nature. They seem tireless as they go about the business of building their homes, feeding their families, and heading off to work each day. I am not sure what it is about these fascinating, minute creatures, but I find them irresistible.

The hummingbirds arrive at our home each year like clockwork during the first week of May; nature appears to follow her calendar and a schedule just as we humans do. I busy myself cleaning feeders and preparing the nectar while awaiting their arrival as trees begin to blossom and unfold their beauty, to our sheer delight.

A warmer than usual spring revealed an abundance of hummers this season; nearly twenty fast-moving little feathered friends in all. It appears that we live in a location that is not only an ideal summer home for humans but also for the hummingbird.

Our home is nestled on a hillside densely covered with a magnificent variety of native plants and trees, primarily majestic ponderosa pines. A gentle slope of the hill and a natural pathway meander down seventy feet or so to the North Fork of the Flathead River. As the sun moves around to the west each afternoon, the light sparkles on the river like a million diamonds twinkling on a watery pathway. The sounds of the cold, clear water as it tumbles over the rocks and boulders has the same effect on me as the best instrumental music: it is soothing to my soul.

The setting is ideal for the hummingbird, and the gigantic pine south of my office window is home to several of the birds. They come and go seemingly hundreds of times throughout the day. I watch as they hover over the cascading baskets of flowers I have strategically placed around the house for their enjoyment. Okay, yes, I plant them for our enjoyment too, but without the hummingbirds, the flowers might seem overkill: an ostentatious attempt to decorate an already spectacular landscape that is completely without need of further adornment.

Beyond our decks, within a seven-mile area north and south of home, there are acres upon acres of agriculture with a variety of flowering crops and pollinating plants.

When we were building our home nine years ago, I asked our landscaper to surround the house with flowering shrubs, and to please use an abundance of purple. I love purple flowers! The sight of purple in nature strikes a chord deep inside me, and over the years I have observed it has a similar effect on the hummingbirds.

The yard has matured in time yielding many gorgeous plants. We are surrounded by purple salvia, catmint, miniature lilacs, and lavender. Yellow Stella D' Oro lilies and black-eyed Susans bloom a little later on to greet summer's arrival. I imagine the hummingbirds approach our home as if it were a magnificent feast, a veritable buffet! Observing them, I cannot help but draw comparisons between their behavior and that of humans.

Throughout my career and personal lifetime, I have made a study of the interactions of both myself and those around me. What fascinating creatures we human beings are! It has been amazing to participate in and also stand back to witness my own journey, and those of people close to me. Recognizing how people evolve and grow, or how they choose not to, is most intriguing to me.

Those who are evolving have taken to heart the lessons that have been presented to them along the way, and through every challenge they have found ways to persevere and carry on. Seldom do we understand why we face the lessons we do as we are going through them, but as with most things in life, hindsight almost always brings clarity. Frequently we can draw forward a purpose for those lessons from the past, using the past as a teacher to help us to find strength and improve upon our decision making in the present.

As for those who choose not to be open to life's lessons, I discern that they do all they can to avoid growth and change, and I note their struggle. I am not sure it is ever really possible to avoid change. It is the only constant in life, after all. I suppose one can close the door on each opportunity as it comes up; that would certainly be a way to deal with it. Opportunity presented, change denied. Life becomes narrow when options are limited, however. With curiosity I cannot help but wonder, *Do they not see that they are the only ones who hold the key to their better life?*

Throughout the course of my career, I have had the honor and great privilege to be in a position of influence in the various roles I have held. Without a doubt, I *felt* as influential as an entry-level team member in an organization new to me as I did later as a manager and director responsible for a team. Let's put economics aside for a moment, because I am talking about influence here. It is true that as an entry-level employee, I did not directly influence pay rates, nor did I have the ability to make the decisions that I would later on as a manager. What I was able to influence, however, was the working environment.

My desire to enjoy the work day came with my full awareness that I had complete control over how I felt about my job, the way I handled myself while at work, and the way I responded to situations that presented themselves. I *got* that being happy and content was always an inside job, and therefore it was up to me to create my own positive environment regardless of what might be going on around me to the contrary.

Never one to shy away from accountability, I have always felt a tremendous responsibility to bring as much value as possible to those around me. This is as true in my home life with my family and friends as it is in my career with my colleagues and clients. The value I knew I could bring in those early days of my career was pretty simple stuff: uplift those around me, smile, be kind, give my clients and colleagues the best I had to offer, do high-quality work, help others overcome a struggle, treat them with respect, and share ideas to elevate understanding within the team.

In recent years, my transition from various management roles in the travel and hospitality industry to that of life coach operating my own practice has led to a learning curve that has been, well, curvy. I have found myself right at home writing, teaching, and leading workshops on the interpersonal communication skills that challenge everyone. The work has been some of the most eye-opening and gratifying of my life. It is through this venture that I humbly come before you in the spirit of awakening something within you: your desire to better understand yourself.

By way of self-exploration and self-discovery you will likely begin to see yourself and those around you in a beautiful new light. It is owing to the understanding of ourselves and acceptance of the whole package that we are, *blemishes and all;* that we become better equipped to relate to others in positive new ways.

As a result of my own journey, I find that I have become kinder, and more accepting of myself and everyone around me. Although I continue to strive for personal excellence every day, I no longer expect myself to be perfect. Through a broader understanding of what I believe to be my mission in life, I have deepened my listening and learning skills while becoming more tuned in and engaged overall. I view life as a kick in the pants, and I know that sometimes life kicks me in the pants. *Nothing like a good kick now and then to get things moving!*

As I have opened up to observing life, I have found that often the lessons we most need to learn are presented to us in nature. If we tune in and really pay attention to what is going on in the world around us, these lessons can add profound meaning to our lives, as they help us reflect upon ourselves in ways that may astound us. I have found this to be true in my own life, and in this book I will share a few reflections with you in hopes that you will find them motivating.

Throughout the book, I ask many questions, all designed to get you thinking in the creative, problem-solving side of your brain. My questions may very well lead you to questions of your own. Awesome! For further review there is also a worksheet at the end of each chapter. Take the time to open up and reflect as you find your answers, and see what insights emerge for you in the process.

It is my hope that through sharing what I have picked up over the years, both personally and professionally, I will inspire you to embrace change, to not shy away from struggle, and to know that while what you go through may be difficult at times, through perseverance you will absolutely become a grander version of you!

Let's take flight.

Calliope feathers on the wings of my hopes and my dreams,
To some day fly high in the lavender sky.
A warm wind caresses my face,
And my heart overflows with grace.
The dawn breaks to herald a dazzling new day,
As I hover, zip, zoom, The Hummingbird Way.

Life Lesson One

Have Confidence in Your Ability to Fly

As I watch the Anna's hummingbird I call Flash zip around my house in early spring, in my mind's eye I conjure up a small Cirque du Soleil troupe of performers. The hummers are amazing—aerobatic wonders unlike any other birds. They perform with speed and agility, threading the needle, flying with equal confidence forward or backward through the smallest of openings to reach their intended target.

There are more than 325 recognized hummingbird species in the New World, and the Anna's Hummingbird is one of only three species that are permanent residents of the United States and Canada.

Although Flash's species is not the most colorful of the hummingbirds, he is probably best recognized for his ability to fly fast. During a courtship dive, Flash will climb to more than a hundred feet in the air before swooping toward the ground in a display designed to catch the attention of a nearby female. The wind whistles through his stiff tail feathers as he plunges toward the earth, creating a shrill sound called a sonation for added emphasis. The sonation delivers a resounding message—Look at me! With supreme confidence in his ability to fly, Flash continues to court the lovely lady hummingbird who recently arrived on the scene.

*M*y observations of hummingbirds fascinate me in much the same way my observations of other people have for years.

Within moments of meeting someone new, I generally get a feel for whether or not they are happy, how in tune they are with those around them, or how distracted they are, and what level of confidence they are projecting. From there, I draw on my intuition and life experience to make a few assumptions about the level of success they might be experiencing in their world. The higher the individual's level of liveliness, pep, and pizazz, the more personal and professional success I envision them having. The opposite is also true; when I meet someone who appears apathetic, disengaged, or indifferent, I imagine them struggling in certain aspects of their life.

We all draw our interpretations about others in generally the same way. We may even make up stories unconsciously as a matter of habit. Often we base these stories on other people we know or experiences we have had throughout the course of our lives. We note: *this person reminds me of a person I used to work with, they look like someone I know,* or *I recognize the type of person she is because I had a relative who was just like her.* We try hard to understand each other to prepare ourselves for how we might communicate and deal with one another.

Although interpretations can be useful, be aware that holding them as absolutes might also prevent us from opening up to the natural unfolding of a new relationship. That is, if we have already placed someone in what we believe to be the appropriate "bucket," we may be closed to learning anything more about them. As we all know, people do not easily fit into a bucket. When we remember this, we can view our interpretations as limiting beliefs rather than absolutes and allow our relationships to develop organically.

What do you notice when meeting someone for the first time? From the beginning, you probably observe the way they carry themselves, the way they shake hands, and whether or not they look you in the eye, all before they speak a single word. Much that is unsaid still speaks volumes about how they see themselves in relation to the world around them, and you begin to get a sense of them early on, as they get a sense of you.

We detect whether a person appears shy and introverted, outgoing and extroverted, or perhaps an interesting mash-up of the two attitudes. Someone might appear to enjoy mixing it up with other people but also be quite comfortable on their own. We get impressions from all these behaviors. Later we say, "I really liked that guy" or "There was something about him . . . I couldn't quite put my finger on it, but I did not care for him."

Personality styles and discussions of introverted versus extroverted attitudes aside, the way you carry yourself and the degree of confidence you have in yourself and your abilities are discernible to those around you. Each interaction or exchange we have with another person makes an impact whether we intend it or not; we are quite literally detecting one another's energy level, and getting a sense of each other.

Our observations of others can be useful when we draw correlations to our own lives. When we notice how others interact and present themselves, we can use this as a mirror and ask, "What can I learn here?" This question, and recognizing that we share similarities in some form or another with everyone we meet, will open us up to seeing ourselves in a new light. This does not mean judging ourselves against someone else; rather, we approach the question from the perspective of "What I see in you, I also recognize in me, and I would like to get to know us both better." *Excellent!*

Think now for a moment about how you typically enter a room. Do you envision yourself walking with confidence, head up, making eye contact with others as you proceed around the room? Do you engage people in rapport-building conversation, or are you focused on taking a seat, or quietly blending in as quickly as possible? When you speak about yourself, your contributions, your accomplishments and skills, what spirit are you conveying behind the words you speak? Are you enthusiastic, inspiring, and motivated, or are your words hesitant, unsure, and perhaps even a bit insecure?

> Your chances of success in any undertaking can always be measured by your belief in yourself.
> —Robert Collier

One of the primary reasons I was drawn to becoming a coach was this very topic of self-confidence. I have had the opportunity to meet and work with some amazing and gifted people over the course of my career, although many of them had no idea how extraordinary they were, or at least didn't act as if they did. I have watched as they either deliberately or unintentionally downplayed their roles, their abilities, and their expertise at every opportunity. These same people were later passed over for promotions, raises, and other plum opportunities they were well qualified for largely because of their own inability to impress upon others their outstanding attributes.

I recall sitting in a succession planning meeting with my director several years ago as I brought forth the top candidate for a role I would soon be vacating as I advanced within the company. Much to my dismay, the director had doubts about the candidate and believed her incapable of fulfilling all of the job requirements. Although I was satisfied that she was the one who was best suited for the role, she had failed to convince other leaders in the organization that she was "The One." Fortunately she and I had a couple of months before the transition was to take place, and together we hammered out a plan that would best showcase her work in order to present her to leadership for advancement. In the end, she received the well-deserved promotion and continues to grow and advance in her position today.

What may have begun rather innocuously, with the candidate minimizing her contributions and accomplishments as she was learning her role, developed over time into a full-blown habit of "playing small" at every turn.

Many coaching and mentoring sessions I have conducted over

the years have been anchored in a person's beliefs about who they are and what they see themselves as capable of becoming. Regularly, I share my observations about their talents and strengths, while championing them to open up and more fully express who they are and what they do best. Often, a little infusion of confidence is all that is required to help boost someone over the hurdle of being accustomed to "playing small" and onto the track of "playing big" in their life.

Self-confidence grows through every achievement, and diminishes through every act of self-recrimination. You become what you think about all day long, and therefore it is good to take stock now and then of what your belief system and your unconscious thoughts are saying about you. Ask yourself this question: *"What do I believe I am capable of achieving, and how am I conveying this message to those around me?"*

What does it take to *act with confidence?* It takes recognition that you are going to have self-doubt from time to time which is perfectly normal. Through this recognition you can learn to see those doubts as nothing more than thoughts in your mind, and you can manage those thoughts.

Notice how you feel as you experience thoughts of self-doubt. What do you sense going on within you physically? Perhaps you feel butterflies in your stomach, tightening in your shoulders, a sense of pressure in your head, heaviness in your chest, or something else? These physical sensations are indicators that stress is present, fueled by your own anxiety, which is spurred on by your thoughts.

The good news is that they are just your thoughts, not the "how to" rules for conducting your day or your life. At any time, you are free to choose to connect with new thoughts that are more uplifting and supportive of you and your goals.

In that moment when you begin to feel a rise in tension, indicating the presence of stress, you can mentally and emotionally take a step back and notice the thoughts that drift through your mind. You can call out those thoughts as they are happening, and then, to use a hockey term, "hip-check" them out of your mind. Calling out your thoughts might sound something like this:

Hmmm, right now I notice some self-doubt creeping in. If I allow this line of thought to continue, it will undermine my confidence—and I am not willing to let that happen.

The question then becomes:

What thought can I connect to instead that will make me feel stronger and more confident right now?

Once you have formed a new, more empowering thought, it replaces the old one, helping you release self-doubt and easing any mounting tension. Work through the question until you come up with an answer that feels right for you, and be sure to select appropriate wording that is authentically you, something that would be very natural for you to say to yourself. This is your hip-check! Are you ready? It may be something as simple as:

You've got this!

or

C'mon, c'mon. Just keep going.

The new empowering thought has just slammed the old negative impression out of your mind, leaving you free to refocus on your goal.

It may also work well for you to create a few affirmations, or maybe just one really terrific "go-to" affirmation that you can bring to the front of your mind in any situation where your confidence might be wavering. My personal go-to declaration is:

I am whole, perfect, strong, happy, healthy, harmonious, loving, and prosperous.

What does that leave out? Not much, which is the reason it has become my go-to affirmation! Whenever I perceive self-doubt beginning to wash over me, I quickly and deliberately recall that sentence, either reciting it to myself silently if I'm in a public place, or out loud and proud when I am alone. I generally repeat the affirmation two or three times to clear my head and "get my mind right."

There are a couple of points to take into account about affirmations. They should begin with the words "I am" and be formed in the present tense, in a positive manner. An affirmation is nothing more than a way of saying yes to what you want in your life in the present moment. Any negative words would be counterproductive, as they would only serve to affirm the negative, which you do not want. Make sense? It is important to keep it positive as you compose an affirmation that you like, so you will enjoy recalling it. Get creative and have some fun with the process while you are at it! If you see yourself as a sassy person, make your affirmation sassy too. Not only will you shake off the self-doubt—you might even make yourself laugh out loud when you connect to it! There is nothing quite like laughter to shift your energy. *Right on*!

Notice the feeling you have when you make the shift to this more empowering thought. Do you feel a sense of lightening up, calm, or ease? A kind of settling? It is powerful to shift your energy in this way, and as you create a habit of doing this for yourself, the shift will take place more quickly. It is important to be mindful of your thoughts and not permit self-doubt to occupy space in your mind for lengthy periods of time. When you do, you can almost hear the enthusiasm and excitement draining out of you. Think about it. How enthusiastic and excited can you be when you are full of self-doubt? It is not possible to harbor two opposing ideas at one time, so shine a light of understanding and awareness into the darkest corners of your mind. Through the process of affirmation, you can let the negative thought go while you reaffirm and expand on the positive one.

To help illuminate those dark corners of your mind, ask yourself the following question: *Which of my thoughts most often challenge my self-confidence and keep me from "playing big"?* Reflect for a moment on the kinds of messages you replay to yourself. Are you able to relate to any of the following statements?

- I am Not ready.
- I am Not skilled enough.
- I am Not yet educated enough—just one more class, certification, or degree.
- I am Not able to communicate the way I would like to.
- I am Not expert enough.
- I am Not good enough.
- I do Not want to be viewed as a fool or a fraud.
- I am Not, Not, Not . . . enough.

It may surprise you to learn that we all have some form of these messages replaying in our minds. Although the exact message we hear is unique for each of us, to some degree, the messages share a common theme. They are all variations of *I am not enough.* Review the above list again and see if you can find the underlying *I am not enough* message behind each statement.

Truth be told, we rarely feel one hundred percent confident and ready. Yet until we take the first step and move forward anyway, we can never begin to realize our full potential. Understanding that feelings of anxiety or apprehension are a normal condition we all experience can provide a source of comfort along the way.

Keep in mind that the way you feel about yourself and what you believe you are capable of achieving are far more important than what anyone else thinks you can do. And by the way, *the majority of people around you will underestimate your abilities.* They may do so rather innocently, coming from their own frame of reference based on their fears, and what they believe to be true for themselves while applying it to those around them. With your own best interest in mind, vow to never make the mistake of taking on someone else's beliefs about what you can or cannot accomplish in your lifetime. Promise to never limit yourself in this way. What you can and will achieve is up to you and no one else. Determine instead that you will dig deep within yourself and act boldly. Take whatever it is that you want to bring about, combine it with *I believe I can,* and fuel it with focus, dedication, and self-discipline to unleash an unstoppable driving force in your life.

Now that you have addressed the confidence-draining *I am not enough* messages that replay in your mind, and you understand that your belief in yourself is critical to your success, what more can you do? You can give yourself credit for what you have already accomplished with an eye toward parlaying those successes into something more. Make a list of your past accomplishments and use it as your own personal *Realization Register*—dare I say a *feather in your cap?!* Yes—*ta da!* Use this as a reference tool when you need a little reminder of what you know you can achieve—because, undeniably, you already have.

Each *feather in your cap* will serve as a reminder of the successes you have previously enjoyed further underscoring what you can achieve through focus and determination. Of course, you already know what you are capable of accomplishing, but how readily are you drawing on those past successes to give yourself a needed boost when you sense self-doubt lurking around the corner? Imagine the feeling of confidence you will gain as you look at all of your accomplishments, small and large. And appreciate that everything on that list was once a *"to do"* before it was a *"ta da!" Pretty cool, huh?*

Consider both personal and professional accomplishments for your list, and feel free to go back as far as necessary in the past to account for all that is significant to you. Try to recall earned certifications, awards, medals, and ribbons. What positive new habits did you cultivate? How about any tired old habits you discontinued that were no longer serving you; think of those as successes too, and jot them down. Have you learned any new skills, increased your abilities, or enhanced yourself further in some way? Now you're on a roll. List the contests you have won, challenges you have overcome, promotions you earned, and the personal or professional recognition you have received that will bolster your energy and your belief in yourself.

Use your past successes as the foundation building blocks to create more of what you want and *grow confident in your ability to fly.*

Worksheet One:
Have Confidence in Your Ability to Fly

What activities or interests do you pursue that make you feel great, confident, on track?

_____
_____
_____
_____
_____

What might you do to connect to those feelings of confidence in yourself when you are unsure or uneasy, lacking confidence? Consider tools we have reviewed in this chapter: affirmations, reviewing your Realization Register, and recognizing and replacing negative messaging.

_____
_____
_____
_____

What feelings do you have about the importance of the role you play in your work?

_____
_____
_____
_____
_____

How do these feelings impact your confidence at work?

_____
_____
_____
_____
_____

On a scale of 1 to 10, how confident are you in the way you are currently managing your relationships?

_____
_____
_____
_____
_____

What would have to happen for you to rate a 9 or 10?

_____
_____
_____
_____
_____

Fine-tune your Realization Register and post it in one or two places where you can easily recall each feather in your cap, and if you are so inclined, feel free to take a bow.

_____

_____

_____

_____

_____

Life Lesson Two

Hover and Rise Above

The warm glow of the rising sun reveals the flower garden, full of life and opening to the presence of the bumblebee effortlessly making its way around the blooming salvia plant. Nearby, sipping salvia nectar while delicately tracing around each blossom, is the male black-chinned hummingbird I call Arthur. The name seems fitting for a hummingbird whose feathered black head, purple neckband, and white chest mimic the appearance of a tuxedo-clad proper English gentleman.

Arthur acquires most of his calories from flower nectar he gathers by using his long bill to reach deep into the flower's funnel while lapping it up with his slender fringed tongue. Since he can only access the funnel from the front of the flower where there is no perch to light on, Arthur's ability to hover is critical to his survival.

Approaching his next anticipated target, Arthur zips in and stabilizes himself, hovering beside me in midair as he surveys the surroundings for potential threats. I stand perfectly still in the midst of the flowering catmint, watering can in hand, and in no time Arthur begins to feed once again.

*T*he hummingbird teaches us that to harmonize with others we should first rise above our current circumstances to gain a fresh perspective on life. Our own ability to stand back and detach from our immediate environment in order to fully absorb what is going on around us is an excellent skill to master, one which, when perfected, can elevate our lives to new heights of achievement and understanding. When we develop the ability to hover like the hummingbird, we are able to metaphorically step outside of ourselves, at times even detaching from our emotions. By doing so we gain a broader perspective and the objectivity required to make better, more fully informed decisions.

It is possible to have a rich and meaningful life without developing this important skill of "hovering," yet there is so much learning to be gained from taking the long and wide view of the situations we find ourselves in.

As a coach, I am regularly called upon to help clients see what is going on in and around their lives, and to bring some added perspective to otherwise confusing situations. Perspective is a funny thing: it is colored by our life experiences both present and past. The way we choose to see ourselves and those around us is also reflected in our perspective. In this way, our perspective can be viewed as what is "true for us." That's true with a small "t," though, because what is true for *any one of us* may not be true for *every one of us*. Another person may have a completely different take on how things are, and what they see may also be "true" for them. Good information to have, right? This brings new understanding to the old adage *"There are two sides to every story, and the truth lies somewhere in the middle."*

I learned my own lessons on perspective and what is true for me early in life. Growing up, my two younger sisters and I shared many experiences, yet rarely did the three of us agree on what transpired while we were together. How could this be? Three sisters, all very close in age, sharing an experience of the same place and time and yet coming away from it with different perspectives—that was fascinating to me. As unique individuals we saw our experiences through the filters of our own lives, and found what was "true" for us through that filter.

> Everything we hear is an opinion, not a fact. Everything we
> see is a perspective, not the truth.
> —Marcus Aurelius

Life is like that for all of us. The ways in which we view situations, other people, and the world at large are reflections of how we see our own lives in relation to what is going on around us. We are constantly interpreting thoughts about what and who we are as we experience everything through a filter that is as unique as we are. *No wonder it is difficult to understand each other from time to time!* If only we all came equipped with a personal playbook, a manual, or How to Best Relate to Each Other instructions!

Consider for a moment how forms of interpretation take shape in the work environment. The he-said, she-said phenomenon unfolds all day long, and in many ways as we are so wrapped up in our interpretations of events that we simply cannot get out of our own way long enough to clearly and objectively see what is actually going on. Precious time and energy are wasted trying to convince others of our point of view rather than accepting our differences for the purpose of seeking common ground in our work together.

How, then, do we use the lesson of the hummingbird to hover and rise above our own frame of reference so we can clearly see all of the available perspectives in front of us?

First and foremost, we can *lighten up and stop taking everything so personally.* When someone shares an opinion that differs from ours, it does not mean they are questioning our integrity, or attacking us personally. Instead of viewing situations as me versus you, as in *"You are with me or you are against me,"* we can choose the outlook that we might simply have different understandings based on our unique perspectives. Internally, that thought process will feel less threatening, which will enable us to be more open-minded and tolerant of one another, more capable of considering another viewpoint.

Once we are aware that we have the ability to both participate in and observe what is happening in our own lives, we can make a choice. We may notice that we are standing fast in our current position, like a statue, unable to move. Or perhaps we observe that we are in a situation that is wrought with emotion, and we notice that we are not thinking clearly because we are attached to a certain outcome or expectation.

In this time of recognition, we can take our cue from Arthur the hummingbird to stop mid-flight while we hover, observe our circumstances, and ask ourselves:

What is going on with me in this moment?
Why am I feeling so emotionally charged?
What might I be overlooking here?
How might I view this situation from another perspective?

With this added insight and consideration we have created a little mental space, some breathing room. It is as though we have stepped into the space between stimulus and response. In that space, we can experience the thoughts and emotions that come through us while discerning that we are not those thoughts and emotions. At any time, we can choose new thoughts and adopt new perspectives simply by choosing to do so. Cool!

This ability to broaden our perspective and intentionally shift our outlook so we can see things differently can carry us a long way toward success in our communication and relationships. Imagine how challenges can be transformed when we take the birds' eye view to entertain new perspectives and new ways of looking at old problems.

Think about a challenge that you have faced recently, and try to recall the way you worked through it. How might you have applied the skill of rising above your own experience to act as both observer and participant in that interaction? What might developing this skill of *hovering* make possible in the future?

Your newfound ability to *hover*—observing your interactions while simultaneously participating in them—will allow you to establish new perspectives that may help you break the patterns of the past. Think of it this way: if you tend to respond in a certain way to a given situation, because that is the way you always respond, you already know the minute the scene begins to unfold what you will do and the outcome that will result. No big surprise there. The outcome is, on the whole, virtually the same each time. This is especially true when you are dealing with people with whom you are very familiar. Think of the way you typically interact with your spouse, parents, children, coworkers, boss, and friends.

If there is an issue in your life that you would like to change or elevate in some way, try adopting a new approach in order to reach a new outcome. What would it take for you to be more nimble, more flexible, or more maneuverable within your relationships?

What lesson can we glean from the hummingbird's maneuverability? In relationships, when one person changes direction, and shows up differently, the relationship *becomes different* as the familiar patterns of flight or fight change. Think about it. It will no longer be the standard aerial maneuvers when someone flies in upside down! I bet you are wondering where your own wings are right about now.

Consider a relationship challenge you have with someone close to you. Now, let's zoom in close enough to get a little pollen on us to view this challenge clearly. Picture the endless looping discussion that ensues each time you broach a certain touchy topic. While being present to the conversation you are having, observe the setting as it unfolds. What do you notice about the other person—their energy, emotions, and body language? Do they appear to be animated, upset, or excited? How effectively are they conveying the message they want you to hear? Take note of when emotion is present and what it does to their communication. Would you say emotion is enhancing the process, stifling it, having little affect, or (fill in the blank)?

Next, notice the feelings that are bubbling up for you, and factor in the way you would ordinarily respond based on your emotions. What expectations do you have of the other person, the conversation, and the outcome of the discussion currently under way?

One important note here: it is through our attachment to

specific ideas of what we believe others should say or do that we create emotion within us when those expectations are not met. Ah-ha! *We create our own emotion based on mismatched expectations.* We make ourselves angry, upset, sad, disappointed, frustrated, vexed, stressed, or you name it—we create it! No one else makes us feel anything; we do this to ourselves. Good to know! If we are doing something to upset ourselves, it is fully within our power to *stop* upsetting ourselves. Wahoo!

With this insight we gain an opportunity to see things in a different light. The question becomes: *How might I put aside my own expectations and be receptive to what is unfolding here?* Allowing for this "space" in the conversation, without attachment, will open your mind since you will no longer hold a preconceived or expected outcome. Make sense? Gone will be the mismatched expectations that were stumbling blocks in the past.

Now you get to choose how you will show up in this encounter—and every encounter, for that matter. You always have a choice. When taking into account the kind of person you most want to be, and while representing the highest vision you hold of yourself, how do you choose to respond in this moment? Will you meet the other person with emotion and energy similar to their own, or will you respond in a new way, one that changes everything for the better? What might that look like? How might the relationship pattern of flight or fight change when your hovering changes your perspective?

There is one more point on the issue of rising above it all: if it is important enough for you to evolve in your relationships and elevate them to their greatest potential, it will be necessary to fly away from *the need to be right.* When we need to always be right, we make others wrong, and we have no ability to uplift a situation as long as we cannot let go of this "need." Granted, we may be successful in getting another person to back down or come around to our viewpoint by continuing to press them, again and again, with our message. Yet this is not the same as gaining agreement, and in fact, we may leave them feeling diminished in some way. They may simply decide that it's more important for the well-being of the relationship to concede in order to bring about a peaceful resolution while allowing for the discomfort to end.

There is ego involved in this kind of interaction, and we will explore that topic more in an upcoming chapter, but to continue with the topic of perspective, here is something important to understand: it is possible for two people to see things differently and to *both be right*. When we make it OK to have a difference of opinion, this does not make one of us less valuable or important, and at times, the best solution may be to simply agree to disagree and leave it at that.

When we entertain the idea that there may be a grain of truth in every point of view, we open our minds to seeing things differently and enhance our ability to learn something new. When the mind is open, an open heart often follows, and this creates room for acceptance of our differences. Acceptance, like Arthur and the bumblebee side by side living their life purpose in total harmony with one another.

Acceptance and harmony: two elegant principles to build on. Would you agree?

Worksheet Two:
Hover and Rise Above

What is true for you? (Emphasis on small "t.") Describe what you think is true about your life, your family, your work, your past, your reality, your hopes, your dreams, and your future.

_____

_____

_____

_____

_____

When you discover that you have been triggered, and you're amped up and on edge in a conversation or interaction with another person, how do you normally react? (For example, I typically withdraw and become silent, walk out, get defensive, or make a "snarky" comment.)

_____

_____

_____

_____

_____

Considering your normal reactions, where might attachment to
a certain outcome play a role? (As an example, I am attached
to the expectation of the outcome that I will always be treated
with respect by everyone.)

_____

_____

_____

_____

_____

When you're amped up, what benefits would there be for you to
"hover and rise above," taking a broad view of life?

_____

_____

_____

_____

_____

How can you develop the skill of being aware that you are both
the observer and the participant in the present moment?
(For example, you might take a deep breath and recall that
we each have a unique perspective, or you could picture
yourself picking up your box of expectations and setting
them off to one side.)

_____

_____

_____

_____

_____

What one skill would you like to cultivate to elevate your relationship with yourself and those around you? (For example, you
may want to let go of the need to have the last word. Or you
might like to develop the ability to have conversations in which
you are open to all that happens without thoughts about how
these interactions should unfold.)

_____

_____

_____

_____

_____

Life Lesson Three

Bare Your Feathers

Hovering in a lustrous sunbeam, appearing to magically pause in thin air, Flicker, the broad-tailed hummingbird aims her needlelike beak into the center of the cone shaped flower, half disappearing as she enters it. Flicker appears unconcerned as she bares her feathers blissfully, revealing her nature exactly as it is, floating in her vulnerability. Instinctively she knows what she values most, and the order in which her values play out in her life. First and foremost, I imagine the hummer must value her ability to fly in every direction. She must also value speed, safety, freedom from predators, a little sweet nectar, and a warm feathered nest. I watch her backing out of the flower, and I giggle imagining Flicker also values having her face covered in pollen.

*I*magine yourself, feathers bared like the hummingbird. Think for a moment about what is going on inside you, and what it is that you value most in life. You may find thoughts stirring about how much it means to have good health, a loving family, great relationships, a stable home environment, or steady employment. Perhaps other ideas came to mind that you value equally—but do you really value everything equally? Chances are that you do not. There is likely an order to the priorities in your life that you may not even be consciously aware of. A quick internet search can lead you to a variety of tools for your use in clarifying your values, but let's take it a step further to delve into what *really makes you tick*. What I synthesized from the values exploration during the iPEC coach training program was the deeper significance of uncovering your *Top Core Values—core values are the master key to unlock your self-discovery!*

Are you ready to discover your core values? Let's get started!

If I were to ask you what your *Top Five Core Values* are, what would you say? Are your core values on the tip of your tongue, easy to rattle off, or are they something you rarely give any thought to? Perhaps you can recall a couple of things you deeply value but you are unsure what your top five might be. You may even be asking, *Why is this important, anyway? I have come this far in life, and not having defined my core values hasn't seemed to hurt me, so what is the big deal?* Great question!

Have you ever found yourself in a position where you needed to make a tough decision and were really struggling with it? Maybe you recall trying to weigh the pros and cons of that decision to the best of your ability while still feeling a bit at a loss. It may be that you made your decision and found that you had regrets afterward, or that it just did not feel right, or that the consequences of your decision impacted your life in a way you had not considered. What might have happened during the process of deciding?

When we have a clear understanding of what our top core values are, decisions become easier. That does not mean that you no longer have tough decisions to make, but rather, that the decision-making process should be easier for you. No longer are you likely to wrestle with your thoughts, or feel like you are completely in the dark as to where to begin. Instead of asking yourself, *Should I or shouldn't I?* the questions become *What core value might this decision impact?* and *How will this decision align me with my core values?* Fully considering the way a decision either aligns with or falls away from what you most value in your *heart of hearts* brings clarity to even the most difficult decisions. After all, your core values are your internal beliefs, those driving forces that define the way you live your life.

When the decisions you make and the beliefs you hold through your core values are in alignment, you will feel that your life works pretty well. This is not to say that it will all be smooth sailing, but you will feel to a large degree that your life is on the right track. On the contrary, when the decisions you make go against your core values, you will feel that you are *derailed,* and life is *off track.* You may have chosen to go against a core value but did so knowing the consequences because you were willing to pay the price. That happens sometimes.

For example, the person who has a core value of *Flexibility* and leaves their role as a freelance writer to take a high-paying job at a magazine with a strict 8 a.m. to 5 p.m. weekly work schedule may feel off track with that decision. Yet if that same person also holds *Financial Security* as a core value, they have consciously considered one core value against another when making their decision. *Financial Security* took precedence over *Flexibility* in this instance.

Here is where the way values may play out gets interesting. Say this person highly values *Flexibility,* but *Financial Security* is their number-one core value and therefore often takes precedence when they make a decision. If *Financial Security* is not being met, this person will feel challenged and out of balance, as if their entire life is out of whack and not working for them. When that top core value is then honored and *Financial Security* stabilizes, all other values will fall in line behind it at varying degrees of importance. Since *Flexibility* is not number one but is still a core value, this person may continue to seek ways to build *Flexibility* into their career somehow while maintaining overall satisfaction with the decision they made.

If in this example the core values were reversed and the person placed *Flexibility* as their top core value over *Financial Security,* they may feel that they have "sold out" on that top core value by giving up their freelance role and accepting a regimented weekly work schedule and regular pay. Think of the person who says, "I sold out my dreams in order to put food on the table." In this case, rather than enduring a lifetime of feeling miserable about the decision they made, they need only to find a great way to "reframe" this internal message. Although they value *Flexibility,* they may also realize that in truth they had very little of it because they couldn't pay their bills, and they had lost control over their daily schedule as a result. With this in mind rather than replaying the message of "I sold out my dreams," they can choose to reframe their choice in a way that makes them feel far better about it. For example, "I traded *Flexibility* in my *daily schedule* for *Flexibility* in my *life,* brought about by the newfound freedoms of financial security. I now exercise *Flexibility* in the way I spend my money, the type of house I live in, the type of car I drive, and the vacations I can now afford to take." What a difference a positive reframe can make! Simply by changing the way we choose to look at a situation, we can elevate the outcome.

It is useful to know your top core values not only because you can base your decisions on what is most important to you, but also because you can start to look for ways in which your environment and the people in it are in alignment with you and your core values. If you value *Integrity* but spend the majority of your time with people who play *fast and loose* with moral principles, chances are you will feel pretty crummy as a result. When you sense that your life is *off track* in any area, it is time to look at your core values and determine where you might have fallen out of alignment with them.

Men acquire a particular quality by constantly acting in a
particular way.
—Aristotle

Are you ready to get clear on what your core values are? The
worksheet at the end of this chapter contains a list of positive values,
many of which may appeal to you on one level or another. Review
the list a few times as you consider what your core values might be.
Circle your *Top Five Core Values* and then number them in their order of importance. Feel free to write in a different value if you do not
find yours listed here. Resist the temptation to circle ten or twenty
values because you think they all sound good. That will not help
you find clarity around what you hold most important; you want
to define the top values. If you feel torn, hold one value up against
another and consider how you make your decisions. Which is most
important? Think about your top values as those that are "nonnego-
tiable" or "must have," without which life does not work very well.
This should help you to get clear.

Worksheet Three:
Bare Your Feathers

Consider the following core values. Which are most important to you? Which are your "non negotiables?" Choose your top five.

Abundance	Concern
Achievement	Courage
Accountability	Creativity
Adaptability	Dependability
Adventure	Determination
Altruism	Emotional Health
Appreciation	Encouragement
Assertiveness	Excellence
Authenticity	Faith
Balance	Family
Beauty	Financial Security
Benevolence	Flexibility
Caring	Freedom
Charity	Friendship
Clarity	Fun
Collaboration	Generosity
Commitment	Goodness
Community	Gratitude

Honesty	Reliability
Humor	Respect
Individuality	Responsibility
Integrity	Security
Joy	Self-care
Leadership	Self-discovery
Loyalty	Self-expression
Marriage	Self-realization
Nature	Self-mastery
Openness	Service
Optimism	Spirituality
Partnership	Strength
Patience	Tolerance
Personal Growth	Trustworthy
Physical Appearance	Virtue
Privacy	Vitality
Professionalism	Walking the Talk
Recognition	

With your Top Five Values in hand, over the course of the next several days or weeks, regularly refer to your list as you entertain the following questions:

- What values am I honoring right now?
- What values are being challenged?
- What has to happen in order for me to live in alignment with my values every day?
- What insight have I gained through this process of getting clear on my core values?

Life Lesson Four

Be Industrious

I sit quietly in the sun-drenched window seat of our great room so I can keep an eye on a broad-tailed hummingbird flying near a large basket of assorted flowers that graces our front doorway, and I watch as he hovers over stem after stem, pollinating as he goes.

If hummingbirds have a personality type, I imagine them to be Type A, just like me. As dynamic and energetic little achievers, hummers appear constantly on the move. During normal flight or while hovering, their tiny wings flutter continuously from twelve to eighty beats per second, creating a rhythmic humming sound evocative of the bumblebee and other insects. Hummingbird wing movement is incredibly fast: up to fifty times faster than the rate of other bird species.

Briefly, the hummer settles on a petunia sprig, and I wonder, Will the flower hold his weight? Tiny as he is, the bow is bending, and then suddenly—he is off! It is back to work for the hummingbird.

*C*hances are that you have heard it said that the only place success comes before work is in the dictionary. How true that is. Even those who appear to have achieved overnight success likely worked long and hard at their craft behind the scenes for years to accomplish those achievements. Clients often ask me what I think they need to do to get ahead and be successful at work. This generally translates into one or more of the following questions:

How can I gain control of my day despite the constant interruptions?
How can I make more money?
What can I do to get promoted?

Industrious at Work

One thing I know for sure is that businesses do not promote people just because they have put in their time. Now, I should qualify this by saying that I do not pretend to know anything about union or government employment, and I will not attempt to delve into how seniority-based employment works. Drawing on nearly thirty years of experience working for organizations large and small, primarily in the hospitality, travel, and tourism industry, I will share what I have become versed in as a result.

As an organizational leader, I spent a great deal of time training and developing employees to prepare them to advance within their company. Many of those employees were hungry for the knowledge, and they did all they could to prepare themselves for the next opportunity. Other employees did little to grow and develop their skills and expertise, and they became frustrated when they were passed over for advancement. Their response was generally some version of "How could this happen to me? *I* have been here longer than *she* has."

The lesson here is a simple one: *Time in a position has nothing to do with your ability to advance on the job. What you do with your time in a position has everything to do with it.*

As with most everything in life, you must first do the work before you can reap the benefits. That work is not just completing tasks and daily job requirements as expected; it is also finding ways to bring more value to those around you.

Think about the ways in which you can use the lesson of the hummingbird to Be Industrious in your work.

Although I fully understand the eagerness to have it all now, let's be realistic and acknowledge the fact that we are entitled to what we work for, and that is about it. We can believe that we will reap wonderful benefits while at the same time taking the actions needed to bring ourselves into alignment with what we want to achieve and become.

In your current role, you may begin by looking for significant ways to contribute that will get your work noticed. Before you will be rewarded with advancement, it only stands to reason that you must first exceed expectations for the job you are doing now. Bloom where you are planted, and then outgrow the job. How? Through mastery of the work: becoming an expert in it, a problem solver, a customer service genius, a technical whiz, or a key "go to" person. In short, do a stellar job by going beyond what is expected of you, right where you are.

With one eye on the future, you can look for and find new ways to grow your skills and expertise. As you do, opportunities will continue to unfold. Always subscribe to the fact that it is your responsibility to advance your abilities, and no one else is duty-bound to make this happen for you. If you are waiting for your employer to seek additional training classes so you can increase your value, stop waiting and start researching what you can do on your own, right here, right now. If you are unsure what it might take to advance yourself, hire a coach or ask leaders within your organization or your professional connections for some career guidance. What areas of improvement do they see for you and how might you apply yourself to those areas?

Consider courses being offered, for credit or not, through community colleges or universities. Many such courses are available both on site and online, making it easier now than ever before to get that next degree or additional certification. Perhaps you have trouble speaking or effectively communicating with colleagues or customers. If so, a speakers' organization or club like Toastmasters International might be beneficial. In addition to any professional guidance such as this that you might require, also take the time to assess where you are personally. Take a look at the complete picture of who you are, and consider what you need to move closer to your ideal vision of who you want to be on the job. Invest in the time to practice and perfect your skills through a variety of additional training and education. The work you do on yourself will ultimately lead to further realization and achievement benefiting all facets of your life.

Next, take a look at the processes involved in your work. How are you at handling the basic organizational tasks and requirements of your job? Do you work efficiently and effectively, making good use of the hours you are at work? What type of colleague are you? Are you highly engaged and a positive contributor to your organization, up and down the ladder? How effective are you with customers?

Following are three mock employee groups that I created for illustration purposes. Of course, I have painted with very broad brushstrokes here, but they share characteristics with employees I often encountered in my role as a leader. See if you recognize any of them.

I think of the first type as the "Steady Eddies." They are ever eager to learn their roles and become very comfortable with their day-to-day tasks. They are skilled on the computer, competent in dealing with customers, and knowledgeable about the company's products or services. Steady Eddies are adept at getting "in the zone" and working productively throughout the day. Solid as a rock, these people are a plus to have on any team. The challenge for Steady Eddies comes when anything out of the ordinary happens; if it does, their productivity slides. Change itself is problematic—it can rock their world—making it difficult for them to get back on task, put the situation behind them, and return to their normal level of productivity. Steady Eddies are generally interested in additional training only if it directly serves the purpose of the work they are currently doing, it takes place during work hours, and they do not have to pay for it.

Our second group is the "Bring-it-on Bettys." These are the high achievers, the risk takers, the "I am up for the task and want to move ahead" employees. Problems do not throw them; they often enjoy the variety that challenges bring to their day and view the change of pace as a blessing rather than a curse. Their unflappability in the face of adversity often attracts the notice of supervisors and managers. Many are groomed as team leaders with an eye toward their future development. The challenges with these employees are often the opposite of those posed by the Steady Eddies. Bring-it-on-Bettys are easily bored. They require variety in their work, ongoing training, and regular development with opportunities to advance, or their employers risk losing them.

Third are the "Five O'clock Freddies." Regardless of what is happening around them, Freddies watch the clock, and when the big hand is on the 12 and the little hand is on the 5, they are already halfway down the block. I am happy to say I had limited exposure to those employees over the years. Typically, they do the minimum required to get by and seldom work well in a team environment. Those around them quickly learn that while Freddies will take all of the help they can get when they need it, they are unwilling to return the favor. Employees like this can be a handful. Lacking a sense of fair play, they generally opt for a "me first" approach that can be detrimental to morale in the workplace. The last thing an employer wants is a staff full of self-serving, clock-watching employees doing the least amount of work they can to draw a paycheck, and just how well do you suppose the Freddies treat customers?

Which of these three types of employees most remind you of yourself? Maybe you are not an employee at all but a small business owner or entrepreneur. Regardless of who you are working for—yourself or someone else—*how* do you do the work you do? Are you "in the zone" like Steady Eddy, "bring it on" like Betty, or "watching the clock" and doing the minimum to get by like Five O'Clock

Freddy? With this added insight, what might you do differently to improve your results moving forward?

On the personal front, when people face challenges in their work, it frequently carries over to their home environment, and vice versa. Coaching clients often come to our sessions with an issue they believe is "just a work issue," sooner or later through the coaching process they begin to see how the way they think and the beliefs they have adopted about themselves and those around them shape their lives on all fronts: at work and at home.

If you feel you have been passed over for advancement or financial reward at work, or treated unfairly in some way, take the time to honestly assess the situation. Think through what you may have been doing—or not doing—that contributed to the outcome you are currently experiencing. It may also be helpful to get feedback from your colleagues and supervisor in the form of a 360 Review (a common corporate performance review process involving the whole team) or another kind of formal assessment to gain a complete picture.

We all like to believe we are great at leaving work issues at work and home issues at home, or that we are only disorganized at home and we have it all together at the office. In reality we are one person, and rarely can an individual be successful "checking it" at the door. Perhaps you have heard it said that "how we do anything is how we do everything?" That statement is worth pondering closely to see if it applies in any way to you. What affects us in one area of our lives, we generally pack around with us wherever we go, like a crushed suitcase with one crazy wheel that no longer spins in tandem with the others. We cannot seem to roll with it.

We have to take full responsibility for our actions and our own success. When we do that, we accept that we are the ones responsible for changing if our life is not what we had hoped it to be. If we own that we determine our level of engagement in our work and in our learning and personal development, we no longer have an excuse for passively sitting back and waiting for change to occur on our behalf. If we do not make it happen, it simply will not come to pass for us.

Industrious at Home

What does it mean to be industrious at home? It means keeping things clean, organized, and running super smooth and efficiently. The pride you have in home and family will show in the care you take for your home and those in it. It takes some effort on the part of everyone you live with to maintain an organized household, but the rewards far exceed the work that goes into it.

How important is it to have your home running smoothly? You get to decide. It is only your shelter from the world, after all! I smile here, knowing how much lighter on my toes I feel when my home runs like a well-oiled machine. Keeping it clean, organized, and running efficiently means picking up as I go, paying bills and doing the banking on time, using calendars for our family and business activities so that we keep our schedules and attend to important details. Everything has a place in our home, and very seldom do we need to look for lost articles, files, or other crucial items. It is so essential to create the right environment in your home, one that supports you and your family rather than one that is cluttered and unorganized, draining you of your precious time and energy.

Call to mind the types of support systems you have in place in your home. Do you use a filing system that is easy to use and manage? Do you keep track of banking and bill paying online, updating transactions on a daily basis so it's easy to track expenses against your budget? How about calendars for planning and following family whereabouts? Personally, I found a calendar system immensely helpful in a household where weekly business travel was the norm.

How industrious and efficient are you with the other areas in your home and personal life? Are you organized in your meal planning and keeping an inventory of grocery and home goods, or do you find yourself running to the store numerous times throughout the week for an item here or there? How might you streamline some of the ways you currently manage details at home so you can free up more time to do things like building your skills, furthering your education, or learning a new craft or trade?

Industrious in Relationships

Finally, I just love the idea of applying this lesson of Be Industrious to our relationships.

When we define being industrious as working *energetically and devotedly,* that strikes me as one tremendous platform to build relationships on! How do you express yourself energetically and devotedly in your relationships? You may demonstrate this in your attention to detail when you consider what is of paramount importance to those close to you and do what you can to deliver it—whether through your time, attention, or assistance—in the spirit of caring and cooperation.

How effective are you when it comes to paying attention to others? Do you find yourself distracted, or do you listen intently and fully engaged when others speak to you? Do you allow time for them to share their wisdom and insights, or do you wave them off or finish their sentences because you are short on time?

What improvements might you make in the areas of commitment and communication when you approach them as your most energetic and devoted self?

Whether your focus is to be industrious at work, at home, or in your relationships, when your efforts are meaningful for you, it becomes easy to feel a sense of purpose and give it your all!

Worksheet Four:
Be Industrious

Getting clear on your current state, describe your level of
    engagement and industriousness in the following areas:
    Work _____
    Home _____
    Relationships _____

What gaps exist between your current state and what you see as the
    highest performance you can achieve in each area?
    Work _____
    Home _____
    Relationships _____

What action steps can you perform to overcome the gaps you
    listed above?
    Work _____
    Home _____
    Relationships _____

What obstacles are apt to get in the way of your accomplishing
these action steps?

_____

_____

_____

_____

_____

How will you plan to work over, around, or through those obstacles
you describe above?

_____

_____

_____

_____

_____

What timelines are you willing to commit to in order to complete
these action steps?

Work _____

Home _____

Relationships _____

Life Lesson Five

Fly Steady and True

The sunlight fades across the western sky, marking the end of another magical summer day. Like a master artist showing off his best work, the sun streaks the upper atmosphere with shades of lavender and pale pink. The hummingbird makes his way from feeder to planters and then home to the pines for his final trip of the evening. He appears to conserve his energy by flying with singular purpose, wasting no effort on an indirect approach to any of his intended targets. Seemingly inclined to accomplish more than might be possible for other species, the hummingbird flies tirelessly from sunup to sundown. He appears focused on his mission and his results, demonstrated by the consistency of his true and steady actions.

*H*ow consistent are you in your thoughts, words, and deeds? If you decide to pledge your participation in an endeavor, do you fully consider the consequences? What sort of follow-up do you typically engage in to back your commitments? Are you steady as a rock and right on schedule, demonstrating that your word is your bond or . . . something else?

How would you describe your own character, and how might those around you describe your character based on what they experience of you? The description of your character that others share—what others perceive you to be—is your reputation.

> Character is like a tree and reputation like a shadow. The shadow is what we think of it; the tree is the real thing.
> —Abraham Lincoln

If strong character and a solid reputation are built on honesty, integrity, responsibility, and trust, how do your day-to-day actions either support or fall away from what you intend to portray to yourself and others?

Think back a few years and see if you can recall a time when we lived in a society in which two people agreed on a course of action and that was it—end of story. There were no additional conversations like this:

"Are we still on for Friday?"
"What's up on Friday?"
"Well, you said you were going to work on that project with me."

When you received that commitment for Friday, did you feel it was necessary to reconfirm that what you both agreed upon would still take place? What belief leads you to reconfirm such commitments with others?

By all accounts, there appears to be a new societal norm. Somewhere along the line it became acceptable to overbook, overcommit, and then underdeliver on our promises to others. We regularly take on too much, jamming our lives full and shoehorning our day planners with superfluous activities. Then, later, we feel within our rights to cancel on those commitments. "Well, there is no way I can make that happen. I am far too busy, beyond busy, so very busy," we say.

Let us break down all of the busy-ness for just a minute. What on earth is the deal with us claiming we are crazy busy all of the time? Knowing that we are the ones who have filled our own plates to overflowing, more often than not our claim of busy-ness appears more like a thinly veiled boast disguised as a complaint. "Sorry, I haven't had time for you . . . it has been soooo busy!" Supposing we are not the ones running our lives, then *who* or *what* is? C'mon now. Everything on our schedule is either there because we put it there or because we allowed someone else to.

Moreover, is this need to be doing something every minute of the day truly a testament to our personal success, or is it more of a revelation of our anxieties? Take a minute to contemplate how you relate to this statement: *"If I am not doing something, I must not 'be' something."*

Have you noticed that the normal response to someone's declaration "I am crazy busy" claim has become "Good for you" or "That is a good problem to have!" In not-too-distant years past, we might have responded more along the lines of "Crazy busy? Oh dear, are you alright? Is there something I can do to help?" *Back then we did not view busy-ness as a feather in the cap; rather, we saw it as a problem to overcome, and* with reinforcements if necessary.

Where does the breakdown occur between what we commit to do and what we end up doing?

We generally know that when we agree to take on extra or unwanted activities, we are not likely to follow through, and we can readily recognize others' similar intent when we hear responses such as "I can try to make it." What do we know about an agreement when someone responds with "I can try to make it?" That it is not an agreement at all; the person is not ready or willing to commit to making it happen, and at the same time they are unwilling to say, clearly and definitively, "No."

What else do we know that is as true for us as it is for those around us? *If it is important to us, we will find a way. If it is not, we will find an excuse.*

Many of my clients share that the all too common reason they overcommit to others is that they do not wish to create hard feelings by saying no to a request. Instead, they say yes, viewing this as a way to avoid conflicting with or disappointing someone. What happens later when you find yourself unable or unwilling to keep a commitment? You have a choice to make: cancel, which will cause the very disappointment or conflict you said you didn't want to create in the first place, or keep the commitment and show up even when you don't want to be there. Neither option is ideal.

If you show up but do not wish to be there, what sort of energy are you likely to present to those around you? Have you ever seen someone else do this—show up physically while *checked out* emotionally or mentally? It is as if they're saying, "Sigh . . . I am here, but I have no energy or excitement about this." They're like emotional Hoover vacuum cleaners, sucking the life out of those around them. Decide right now that you will never be the Hoover!

When someone drops a commitment they have made to us, we tend to judge them and their behavior pretty harshly. On the contrary, if we're the ones doing the dropping, we tend to give ourselves a free pass, viewing ourselves favorably anyway based on what we *intended* to do. But whether or not you intended to do something, if you made the agreement and then broke it, you have let someone else down. And whether you realize it or not, you have let yourself down too. You will recognize that you are withdrawing your energy from interactions and not demonstrating solid character by habitually breaking commitments or showing up halfheartedly. It will gnaw at you, that nagging bit of conscience that takes up space in your head.

You may feel a twinge of guilt or just have a sense that there always seems to be fragments of life that you are walking away from.

Choose instead to show up in reassuring ways, demonstrating your personal best in every encounter with another human being. When you give your word and make a commitment to someone, honor it—no matter what! Let others see that they can count on you to be there with *bells on*. Believe that your personal integrity is far too important to compromise, and live from this reality every day.

We Fly Steady and True when we choose to own our actions by firmly expressing "Yes" or "No" with clarity of mind and constancy of character, rather than blaming our inability to keep our commitments on getting caught up in the busy-ness mode. When you stand by your commitments you will recognize what it is like to live the highest possible version of yourself, and you will reinforce your self-esteem rather than undermine it.

Worksheet Five:
Fly Steady and True

Describe your beliefs, feelings, and attitudes as they relate to your image of solid character.

_____

_____

_____

_____

_____

List the attributes you see in yourself and those around you that demonstrate strong character and integrity.

_____

_____

_____

_____

_____

On a scale of 1 to 10, how are you at keeping your commitments to yourself?

_____

To others?

_____

What attributes from the list you created above would you like to
    cultivate to further strengthen your own character?

_____

_____

_____

_____

_____

What actions will you commit to over the course of the next several
    days, weeks, and months to cultivate these strengths?

_____

_____

_____

_____

_____

List the five people you spend the most time with and how the
    character of those individuals impacts your thoughts, beliefs,
    and actions.

_____

_____

_____

_____

_____

Life Lesson Six

Find Your Voice

Early afternoon on mid-summers eve, an adorable and exuberant hummingbird approaches the feeder. I have nicknamed this one "Tucker the Talker" as a tribute to our beloved black Lab, who was also a talker. Tucker the Lab tried hard to communicate in human terms: his funny way of speaking to us was a half-bark, half-moan that he rolled around in his throat to produce a sound similar to the spoken word. The hummer also "speaks" in a chorus of high-pitched chirps, and each time he backs away from the feeder, he continues to "talk." It is a guaranteed crowd pleaser, an instant smile maker, every time Tucker the Talker is near.

*H*ave you found your voice, your special brand of connection to the world around you? If so, how do you express your individuality, your particular creative talents or abilities?

We are all unique and convey our originality in a myriad of ways: singing, cooking, photography, scrapbooking, gardening, writing, making music, and on and on—forever the list goes. Tapping into our creativity is nothing more nor less than being in touch with our core genius. When we are using our imagination, in whatever form it takes, we feel energized and alive, as if we are serving our purpose. That is our core genius at work!

> For his heart was in his work, and the heart giveth grace
> unto every art.
> —Henry Wadsworth Longfellow

Notice how you feel when you are inspired and inventive, drawing from your passion to create something. That is a time when your energy peaks. You are jazzed up, turned on, and operating from your highest self. It is now that you experience an easy joyfulness. Quite simply, you are happy and content for no particular reason. What you love to do comes easily for you—it is your gift! You might think nothing of it: *Ah, it is really no big deal. I am a talented painter, but many people can paint—so what, right?* Well, not so fast!

What you take for granted because it comes easily for you is not necessarily easy for those around you. Many of us keep our gifts under lock and key because we believe that what we have to offer is not "good enough." Yet in truth, anything we do or create from our passion is more than good enough to share with those around us. When you take a leap of faith and open up to share your special brand of genius, your gift becomes a gift to others.

When you consider the form of creativity that makes you feel most alive, what comes to mind? Think about the ways in which you are artistic, clever, imaginative, talented, inspired, or inventive. How do you express these qualities to others?

I have a number of interests that are wonderful outlets for my own creativity. Somewhere along the line, I developed a knack for decorating, and I enjoy feathering our nest. Over the years, my husband and I have had the opportunity to build five new homes, allowing me to hone my decorating skills. Finding just the right furnishings and accessories for the places we have lived in has been fun and rewarding. To finish decorating a place that feels right on, and to hear others share in that feeling by saying, "It is so cozy and comfy at your house," is a supreme compliment to me. Mission accomplished when I make our family and our guests feel a sense of being "at home" in our home.

The yards around our homes have been extensions of the inside space, and I have also cultivated a love of flower gardening and landscaping to further fulfill this desire to decorate.

Another great love of mine is gourmet cooking. My family and friends have all benefited over the years from my willingness to share this passion with them. Now, it is important to note that it was not all beef Wellington, and crab-stuffed Portabella mushroom caps in the beginning. Trust me. I still receive plenty of teasing for my early attempts to be avant garde, cooking up pickle steak and a number of other flops that required a plugged nose and a slug of cold water to get down, but they made me a better cook in the long run.

Over the course of thirty plus years of cooking, I developed an understanding of what flavors meld well by mixing it up and trying new recipes. I also became an early fan of Julia Child, Jacques Pepin, and other professional chefs long before the Food Network craze began. My enthusiasm led me to assemble a collection of gourmet cookbooks, and many years ago my husband, Larry, and I started a weekly Gourmet Night at home, complete with a four- or five-course meal. Everything made from scratch, all unique recipes.

Gourmet Night eventually evolved into Date Night for Larry and me as the boys became teenagers and wanted to spend more time with their friends and less time with their parents on a weekend. I recall one particular Saturday Date Night when we were deep into our meal preparations and the boys' friends started showing up in droves around our kitchen table. We quickly ordered them a few pizzas and returned to our work. Although they were in the family game room, they kept gravitating toward the kitchen. "Gee, Mr. and Mrs. Gerek, it sure smells awesome in here (hint, hint)." Sorry, boys.

The indirect perk from this captivation with cooking has been a close-knit family of cooks who readily exchange recipes, along with lively discussion around our culinary hits and misses. I love it when a family member calls me for ideas on what to make for dinner, or in the heat of the moment will call to say, "Help! My sauce is not coming together. What should I do?" These days it would probably be quicker to Google the answers they are looking for, but they call me anyway. That makes me smile.

I could go on and on about my interests, and I find that I am still trying to figure out how best to combine my love of coaching, writing, cooking, decorating, and travel as the ultimate way for me to express all of the passions I fancy most!

Now let's get back to you . . .

How do you express yourself creatively now? Is there some element of your creativity you are holding back that, if brought to the forefront, might provide further advantages to yourself and others?

You may be quite comfortable expressing your unique brand of gifts while at home or in the presence of loved ones, but would you ever dream of expressing yourself this way in your professional circle? What might be the belief that keeps you from fully expressing your passions and creativity in all areas of your life?

Think about what you can do to stretch outside your comfort zone. You see, the more readily you tap into your core genius, the more "on purpose" you become. While expressing your originality, you should know that you will be functioning at your highest level energetically. Your excitement will come through in all that you do as an overall expression of joy, happiness, and contentment. When you think of yourself working with passion, is there a part of you that resonates with this idea? If you find you are getting motivated at the thought of being on fire in this way, what insights does this provide for you? How might you incorporate more gusto into your personal and professional life so those around you can sense that you are deep in your purpose? Think of a step you can take to regularly spend time expressing yourself through your passion and purpose, wherever you might be.

As an example, if like me you also *love* to cook and enjoy trying new gourmet recipes, where might you begin? Perhaps you could gather inspiration from a few cooking shows, magazines, or websites. You may get some momentum going by adding an assortment of unique spices to your spice rack or picking up a kitchen gadget or two to make meal preparation more pleasurable. Plan to host family or friends for a dinner party featuring a special meal you have prepared as a way to share your creation with others.

Know that what you focus on, you will get good at, and when you have found your own voice, whatever way you choose to express yourself will be absolutely perfect for you.

Worksheet Six:
Find Your Voice

If time and money were no object, what would you choose to spend
time doing that feels most like your true self?

_____

_____

_____

_____

_____

What do you love doing that comes easily and effortlessly to you?

_____

_____

_____

_____

_____

What do others recognize as your strength, and regularly ask for
tips or advice on?

_____

_____

_____

_____

_____

What do you enjoy so much you lose track of time while doing it?

_____

_____

_____

_____

_____

If you get really radical, thinking in a "no limits" way, how might
you take a step in the direction of your greatest passion?

_____

_____

_____

_____

_____

How might you incorporate more of your creativity into your
daily life?

_____

_____

_____

_____

_____

Life Lesson Seven

Take Time to Rest

Even the enterprising hummingbird requires rest between flowers now and then. One sunny morning I stepped out on the front porch, stopped, and stood quietly waiting, believing I had just heard a hummer fly close by. After a moment of hearing nothing more, I took a few steps toward my watering can, which was sitting on a nearby ledge. Suddenly, the husky broad-tailed hummingbird I refer to as Evander, emerged from the center of a hanging planter, came straight toward me, and hovered a few feet away, apparently curious as to what I was up to. Becoming very still so as not to startle him, I returned his curiosity. He hovered a moment longer there, turning 45 degrees in flight, then back 90 degrees, then 90 degrees in the other direction, never losing sight of me. With a gentle twirl and a graceful pirouette, Evander returned to the center of the planter. The little bird was perfectly camouflaged amidst the flowers inside, and I smiled broadly at the sight of him surrounded by exquisite blooms. He tilted his head slightly to get a full look at me and, I suppose, wondered, What on earth is she up to now? I remained where I stood, calm and still, simply enjoying the sight of a little bird at rest before he moved on.

*H*ow in tune are you with your own well-being? When you feel worn out, do you give yourself permission to rest and recharge your batteries? If you are like most people who feel they have too much to do, and too little time in which to do it, you might just keep on pushing yourself.

I can certainly relate to that push! In addition to juggling thirty years of busy careers, Larry and I are also the consummate do-it-yourselfers. Whatever needs to be done around the home or on the property, from minor chores and upkeep to the heavy work of clearing fallen trees and debris from the woods, we do it all, and much of it is hard physical labor. I cannot begin to estimate the cords of wood we have chopped, hauled, and stacked over the years. We have also planted countless trees, flowers, and shrubs of all shapes and sizes. We have hauled and spread tons of rock, cement, and gravel as we constructed retaining walls, walkways, and decks in the variety of homes where we have lived over the years. It was always a labor of love as we devotedly cultivated the grounds around our homes.

The land we live on now was logged at some point before we moved here. The loggers had slashed and burned tons of unwanted debris as they vacated the area, and when we moved in, we were confronted with a mess. Acres of downed trees were left half burned, decayed and rotting in the midst of mature, healthy ponderosa pines and clumps of birch. It took years of hard work to clear the debris and create a fire safety zone around our home, but in the end it was worth the effort. Eventually, what emerged was a magnificent place we are proud to call home.

There were many times along the way when we pushed ourselves to a state of exhaustion, chipping fallen branches, raking, shoveling, hauling, and clearing decayed wood. We commonly spent full evenings in the woods after wrapping up a normal business day and put several hours of the weekend into cleanup work. Often when we finished for the day, we were barely able to transport our tools and equipment back up the hill to the garage. Generally I could be found walking, carrying the light tools, rakes, and shovels while Larry moved tractors, log splitters, and small trailers. It wasn't unusual for us to move directly from the outdoors to the shower and to bed with little time in between.

The notion that you are more productive when you push on after fatigue sets in is not a good one. At a minimum, you are more apt to make mistakes and have to redo subpar work. And when you push the envelope too far physically, the story may end with someone getting hurt. In our case, we had to make a trip to the emergency room after Larry fell off a ladder and cracked several ribs. Other than that, we have been fortunate to remain highly active and healthy despite the occasional strained back, tired muscles, scrapes, splinters, bumps, and bruises.

When it comes to rest, studies have shown that most adults require seven to nine hours of sleep per night to maintain good health. How do you fare in this area? Are you getting adequate rest to support your overall good health? Your body is always sending you signs to let you know whether you are on or off track. When you are not feeling good, tune in and pay close attention to your body. What can you discern from what it is telling you? Are you a little fatigued, pretty drained, or downright exhausted?

For your physical well-being, try to break up your workday with a quick ten-minute walk or a change of scenery every ninety minutes to two hours to recharge your energy. If your surroundings are conducive to walking outdoors, take advantage of the opportunity to allow nature to rejuvenate you. Not only will you benefit physically from the walk, but as a bonus you will also give your mind and spirit a boost by taking in some fresh air and shifting your perspective.

Good for the body is the work of the body, and good for the soul is the work of the soul, and good for either is the work of the other.
—Henry David Thoreau

While at work, create a habit of doing a little stretching periodically to get your blood flowing throughout your system. This will be particularly helpful if you work in a sedentary role, one that has you seated at a desk or standing at a workstation all day.

If you work in a fast-paced environment and you are prone to stress, consider "trying on" a practice of deep breathing several times during your day. Simply shift your focus to your breathing. Take several slow, deep breaths, concentrating on the breath flowing in and out and allowing yourself to clear your mind of the constant stream of thoughts. As thoughts come in, notice them but don't follow them or allow them to lead you anywhere. Just observe your thoughts as they come in and let them pass by as you continue to focus on your breathing. Breathing in this way should help alleviate tension, and it just plain feels good to get the oxygen flowing!

For your mental well-being, rest can take place in any form that makes sense for you and allows you to "power down" to the state of being calm, cool, and collected. Calming music, inspirational or motivational reading, and yoga can also clear the mind of the clutter of the day. Tapping into your creativity or enjoying a few hours of play through fun distractions in a variety of games can be another great way to rest your mind.

What else might you incorporate into your daily practice to bring periods of rest into your day? How might you commit to these practices so that you maintain them, and do not abandon them at some point down the road?

Often when we most need to power down because we have been pushing too hard, we do not give ourselves permission to do so. Instead we push even harder. It is then that we begin to suffer the consequences I mentioned earlier: not doing our best work, feeling ill, or risking injury. Ultimately, we risk burning out. Remember, *even the hummingbird requires rest now and then.* Give yourself permission to take time to rest when you need to, knowing that once you have replenished your energy, you will feel rejuvenated. And you will be better prepared to work once again to your full potential.

Worksheet Seven:
Take Time to Rest

Describe how in tune you are with what you need to do to maintain a healthy mind, body, and spirit.

_____

_____

_____

_____

_____

On a scale of 1 to 10, what is your current level of satisfaction with your physical well-being?

_____

_____

_____

_____

_____

What would it take for you to reach a 9 or 10 on the satisfaction scale?

_____

_____

_____

_____

_____

What activities do you regularly engage in for your physical fitness?

_____

_____

_____

_____

_____

On a scale of 1 to 10, what is your current level of satisfaction with your mental well-being?

_____

_____

_____

_____

_____

What would it take for you to reach a 9 or 10 on the satisfaction scale?

_____

_____

_____

_____

What activities do you regularly engage in for your mental
well-being?

_____

_____

_____

_____

_____

What is your current level of satisfaction, on a scale of 1 to 10,
with your spiritual well-being?

_____

_____

_____

_____

_____

What would it take for you to reach a 9 or 10 on the satisfaction
scale?

_____

_____

_____

_____

_____

How do you replenish your spirit?

_____

_____

_____

_____

_____

Life Lesson Eight

Face Your Fear and Fly Right Through It

Sitting on the back deck on a hot July day, I watch Glo, a female black-chinned hummingbird, dart back and forth as she tries with all her might to reach a feeder that is closely guarded by an aggressive hornet. Each time the hummingbird moves, the hornet matches her with a countermove. This continues for several seconds until the hummingbird darts off toward her home in a ponderosa pine. The hornet follows in hot pursuit, but within seconds Glo is back at the feeder, momentarily alone and feeding once again. The hummingbird must understand that even one small sting from the hornet would be the end of her, yet her desire to drink the nectar is so compelling that she will take a calculated risk to satisfy her craving. The hummer faces her fear head-on and keeps going.

W hat kinds of fears are you facing in your life right now? Are they real and inescapable, fears of things that could bring harm to you in some way if they are not addressed soon? Or are they imagined fears that you are conjuring up in your thoughts?

Think about what is behind an anxiety or a worry that you currently have, and try to view it in a broader perspective so you may rise above it. This is easier said than done when you are experiencing fear. It is hard to be objective when your emotions have been triggered; those surging feelings can become intense, saturate your mental picture, and cloud your thinking. *So,* you may be wondering, *how do I shift to a broader perspective when my thinking is clouded?* Great question!

First, it is useful to recognize that you have shaped many of the fears you face yourself, by interpreting information out of the unknown. This is one of our human specialties, it seems: we just love to scare ourselves half to death with "what if" scenarios. When something comes up and we are apprehensive about it, we create an interpretation or story about it in our mind. We conceive of a number of possible dreadful outcomes, along with other frightening details we do not wish to have happen to us, and we continue to feed our fear by mulling these over . . . and over . . . and over. *Yikes!*

Here is how the shift can happen for you: Think back for a moment to some of the fears you have faced in the past. Recall the strength you drew on then that helped you fly through those challenges. That strength is still within you, a resource you can draw upon at any time you choose. Think about how you might apply it to your current situation. Use your courageous spirit to release that strength from the dark recesses of your mind, and bring it forward once again so it can do you some good. Know that what was true for you in the past can be true for you now.

You also have the ability to calm your fears and alleviate your anxiety simply by challenging your fears and choosing more empowering thoughts.

As a child, I discovered the power that came from challenging fear when it appeared in my own young life. At that time, a little voice in my head regularly told me that I was not good enough—because my parents were divorced, while none of my friends' parents were. In retrospect, it seems silly. Now, with divorce rates being what they are, single-parent families are common. But in 1970, growing up in small town Livingston, Montana, my sisters and I were "different" from the other kids; our situation made us stand out, and not necessarily in a positive way. The little voice in my head was a constant companion back then, always talking to me, always saying, *You can't do that! You're not good enough.* In my mind I would respond, *Oh yeah? I bet I can.* And then I would do whatever the voice said I could not do. I soon noticed that once I did, the little voice disappeared. I imagined it withering, like the Wicked Witch of the West in the scene from *The Wizard of Oz* where Dorothy accidentally doused her with a pail of water. *I'm melting, melting, melting,* my voice would cry out, in the same weak, helpless way. I had won! *Hee hee heeeeeee!* Unbeknownst to me, this was a profound skill to have taught myself as a child, and I would come to understand it more in depth as *Gremlin work* years later while in the iPEC Coach training program.

Early on, I had gathered that my fears were nothing more than a voice in my head, and that I could silence that voice simply by challenging it. This became a game to me—and oh, what fun it was to challenge that voice and fly through my fears! The skill developed then has served me well throughout my lifetime in many ways. It has helped me stretch outside my comfort zone, and to ask for what I want from those around me. Standing up to my fear has also helped me become accustomed to trying new experiences and new ways of thinking. All such actions are more difficult when fear is allowed to run amok and cast its dark shadow over one's life.

*Clouds of fear drift through the imagination. Allowed to lin-
ger, they gather in intensity to invite a storm. Allowed to pass,
through indifference, they scatter and fade with the wind.*

A few years ago our family gathered together in our hometown,
and several of us went out to dinner at the local rib and chop house.
After dinner, as we prepared to leave, we congregated near the restaurant door. As I stood there waiting, I heard a woman call out my
name. It took me a few moments to recognize her as Barb, my first
employer from some thirty years earlier. As I introduced Barb to my
husband, she recalled to us a story of my coming to her at the age
of sixteen to request a raise. She said I told her, "I deserve a raise
based on all of my hard work." I did not recall the conversation she
was sharing, so I asked her if she gave me the raise, and she said,
"Of course! You deserved it!" As we all laughed she went on to say
that in all of her years as a business owner, she had not come across
another kid with the kind of confidence I had demonstrated to her
on that day.

Walking away from the restaurant shortly thereafter, I tried
unsuccessfully to recall my feelings of confidence as a teenager. I
remember being scared silly most of the time as a youngster while,
at the same time, not allowing the scary stuff to stop me from pursu-
ing what I wanted. I am not sure that what I had was confidence: it
felt more like defiance of the ever present fear inducing voice in my
head. Nevertheless, it occurred to me during my encounter with my
former employer that at sixteen years old I was already learning the
skill of negotiation, another ability that has served me well throughout the course of my lifetime.

After I graduated high school and went off to college, a funny
thing happened to that little voice in my head. I noticed it changing—or perhaps it is more accurate to say that I changed *it*. Having
left home for the first time as I ventured out on my own, I experienced a lot of imagined fears. *What was I thinking, picking computer
science as my major? How am I going to make the grades? What if I
fail? How am I supposed to juggle work and studies? I don't want to let
myself or my family down!* The little voice was having a field day with

all of my fears. I was crafting those fears myself, tossing chum into the water while the voice responded like a hungry shark, eating it up and reminding me of even more ways I could fail.

Then one night as I was lying in my dorm room, trying like crazy to overcome a few random fearful thoughts so I could get to sleep, it occurred to me: *Wait a minute. The voice in my head is making me more afraid!* As strange as it may sound, I had a chat with my little voice that very night. I recognized that although it often had something to contribute, offering valuable *words* of caution, there was a problem with *the way* in which it communicated to me. The voice was discouraging—a real killjoy—always seeing the downside, and it was this that made me feel so bad. It was upon this discovery that I had words of my own to share with it: *I want to hear what you have to say, but I will only pay attention when you communicate in a positive way.*

I felt powerful in that moment as I put the little voice on notice! It did not create instantaneous change, as that critical voice was a stubborn one, used to its ways. Over time, however, my little voice transformed into a much more constructive companion. It often comes up with the words of caution, or the question *Are you sure you want to do this?* Yet when it speaks to me now, it appears to have my best interest in mind, and we have worked out a strong partnership together.

I should note that I recognize it would be easy for my little voice to become discouraging again. Unfortunately, its nature is such that it sees the glass half empty, whereas I choose to see it half full. We know these things about each other, and I have noticed that when its talk turns negative, this is more apt to happen when I am not feeling my personal best. This is one reason I take good care of myself, I try to always get plenty of rest, eat healthy foods, and commit to regular exercise. After all, my little voice and I have an agreement, and I do what I can to hold up my end of the bargain.

I may not be wired like most people because I find that I do like to push the envelope. As an adult I have overcome my fear of heights by skydiving and my fear of the ocean by becoming a PADI-certified scuba diver. A few years back, when I was facing the fear associated with thinking it was time to leave the only profession I had ever known to venture out and start my own business, I challenged myself to run a marathon.

Those who know me found this challenge most surprising of all because at the age of forty-six, I had never run a race in my life: not a 10K, a 5K, or a sprint to the end of the block, for that matter. I did not jog or run as a form of exercise. I had never run for any reason beyond the requirements of physical education classes in my youth. I chose to run a marathon because it would be a huge stretch for me: it was truly a transformational goal. I knew that once I had accomplished that, I would be able to muster the courage and the confidence to leave a profession I had progressed in for more than twenty-five years.

For whatever reason, I have found that developing myself physically tends to get me moving mentally. After eight months of training alongside my game-for-anything husband, Larry, I completed all 26.2 glorious marathon miles. I was by no means fast, and the phone did not start ringing off the hook with Boston and LA calling to see if I would please participate in their marathons. But that was never my goal. My goal was to finish ahead of the truck that picked up the cones on the race track, and that I did. With the completed marathon in my history books, I went on to open Let's Strut Your Stuff, and began doing the work I was born to do as a coach.

What are some of the ways you would like to challenge yourself to grow? It does not have to be anything physical. Perhaps you desire to take some art classes, get your pilot's license, return to college, write a book, or earn a professional certification of some kind. When you choose to better yourself—become more skilled, more physically fit, and better educated—you increase your value in the marketplace, and you build your own self-esteem in the process.

Whatever it is that you want to do, the way to gain experience and bolster your self-confidence is by facing your fears head-on so you can develop through them. Take a chance on that initial scary first step! One step is all it takes to get you moving in the direction of your dreams, and with that first step behind you, before you know it—you will be making excellent progress.

As a final thought, consider the many worries and fears you

have had in your life that never came to pass. How might your 20/20 hindsight about those fears help you alleviate any present fears you might be experiencing? You have tremendous resources inside you, and tapping those resources will rouse the personal power necessary to overcome any unfounded fears in your life. Ready? Be brave, and then—prepare to astonish yourself!

Worksheet Eight:
Face Your Fear and Fly Right Through It

What fears do you see as holding you back from becoming the best
possible version of yourself?

_____
_____
_____
_____
_____

What would it take to challenge that fear so you can move forward?

_____
_____
_____
_____
_____

When fear wells up in you, what is the message you replay in
your mind?

_____

_____

_____

_____

_____

What thought might you connect to when you are conjuring up
a fear, in order to move past it and take the next step?

_____

_____

_____

_____

_____

Life Lesson Nine

Every Feather in Place

Each season I look forward to the arrival of the Calliope Hummingbird, who—true to his shy, reserved nature—shows up quietly on the scene. As the smallest North American species of hummer, Calliope is diminutive in stature even by hummingbird standards, measuring only three inches long when fully grown. Despite his wee size, he is always dressed to the nines with exquisite, intricate feathers that he dons like a cloak of smoky gray and emerald green. His crowning glory is his gorget, a collar of dazzling magenta feathers that color him the most impeccably dressed bird at the feeder.

*M*uch of what we explore in *The Hummingbird Way* is our inward reflection of ourselves. Now let's take a look at our outward reflection.

How do you see yourself physically showing up in the world? What sort of presence would you say you have? Would you say your physical being and the way you portray yourself through your attire are in alignment with who you aspire to be? How might your mindset play a role in this portrayal of you? Do you believe it supports you and propels you forward or holds you back?

Most people go to some trouble to get dressed and ready for special occasions. Think through how you normally prepare to attend a wedding, go out to dinner, or be present for any other event that is not a regular happening. With a special event in mind, we take the time and make the effort to select the right garments to wear, choose the right shoes, and add appropriate accessories. We take extra care with our personal grooming, and overall appearance, with the knowledge that we have only one chance to make a great first impression!

Aside from special occasions, how do you wish to represent yourself to the rest of the world? Do you view your go-to choices for your wardrobe as getting high marks in comfort but low marks in presentation? Or worse, maybe when wearing your favorite clothes in public, you risk having your photo taken for a women's magazine, complete with face blocked out and a big red circle with a line through it: fashion blooper! If you can relate to that possibility, it might be time to revamp your outward expression of yourself.

I have never been much of a shopper, although I do enjoy wearing nice clothes, shoes, and accessories. My approach to shopping has always been "get in, get what you need, and get out." You will never find me aimlessly wandering around the mall from store to store, trying on a million articles in order to find that one perfect blouse. And understand that I am in no way advocating that you purchase a new wardrobe. This lesson, Every Feather in Place, is about you portraying yourself outwardly in a way that fully express-es your own best vision of who you choose to be. You may already have all you need in order to do just that, and with a little inspira-tion, you can express yourself in a way that is picture perfect for you!

By now, I hope you are getting the sense that all things in our lives are related to one another. The way we think affects the way we feel, and the way we feel affects the way we act. And here is some-thing more to think about: the way you express yourself through your attire, your personal grooming, and your overall level of care for your physical self is also a message to yourself and those around you. In the words of Ralph Waldo Emerson, "What you are speaks so loudly, I cannot hear what it is you say."

A healthy degree of self-confidence and a positive outlook on life translate directly to taking good care of ourselves and always presenting ourselves in the best possible light.

The opposite is also true. Think about it for a moment. Do you recognize people who are untidy in their appearance, haphazard in their personal grooming, and disheveled as people who have their act together? On the contrary, by appearance alone we garner that they probably don't manage themselves very well.

Taking a cue from their appearance, we can imagine that there are likely other areas they might not care for as they should or could. To take this one step further, if I am an employer interviewing per-spective job candidates for my team, I would notice a disheveled, unkempt person and envision an untidy work space, incomplete projects, and lost files: further I would get a sense of some of the chaos I might bring into the work place if this person were added to the team. More than likely I would pass them over while continuing to search for other candidates who appear to have it together, and whom I would presume to be more suitable

Subconsciously we can relate to someone who appears dishev-eled or unkempt because we know what it is like to not take care of ourselves when we are tired, under the weather, or in some oth-er way just not up to the task. In essence, we see ourselves in this person as we consider a variety of interpretations about what might be going on to put them in this state.

Should you think it is not important to pay attention to the details of how you present yourself, realize that others make assumptions about you all the time based on your personal presentation and appearance. They think: This person cares or they do not; they make a good impression or they do not; they are energetic or they are not; they would make a suitable representative of our group out in the community or they would not.

Perhaps you are now reminded of hearing at an early age the words, *never judge a book by its cover.* Of course, we all know that everybody has more depth of character than we can ascertain from observing them visually. Still, the fact remains that we do use visual perception as a way to gather information. What else do we have to go on when we know little about another person, or when we have had little exposure to them, as when meeting them for the first time? Continuing with the book metaphor, the only narrative some receive is our *book cover.* Therefore, we should take into account the story we wish to impart whether it's told by the entire contents of our book from *Once Upon a Time* through *Happily Ever After* or by the cover only.

What does it take to have Every Feather in Place? It takes clean, well-tailored, well-cared-for clothing that is stylish without necessarily being trendy. Stylish clothing has staying power, whereas trendy clothing has a look that comes and goes out of fashion. You likely do not want to be stuck with a wardrobe of trendy articles unless you are in a position to update your wardrobe on a regular schedule. Classic, stylish clothing rarely goes out of style and can often be made brand new with updated, colorful accessories, or layers.

Strive for the appropriate hairstyle, makeup, and accessories for your particular profession or walk of life. An appropriate hairstyle in a professional office environment can differ greatly from what is appropriate in a creative environment. You have to know what the standard expectations are for your particular surroundings and then harmonize with them. This does not mean you cannot be a maverick and have your own style: of course you can and should have your own style! Just keep in mind the kind of statement you hope to make with "your look." Are you going for "Wow, that look really enhances her professional presence" or "Oh my! Did you see what she is wearing now?" *I know that you know what I am getting at here.* If you are trying to make a statement to elevate your presence and not detract from it, I recommend a slightly more conservative approach. As a general rule of thumb, you might consider this advice: *When in doubt, don't wear it out.*

Your ability to dress for success should also take into account your overall level of health and fitness. If you are conscious of your physical health and take proper care to maintain it, you already project strength, vitality, and high energy to those around you. When you feel good, it shows up as a positive attitude and that little something extra I like to call "sparkle"! With sparkle you exhibit confidence in the way you carry yourself, speak, and act. *Marvelous!*

If you find you are unhealthy, out of shape, or overweight, it is likely you do not feel good physically as a result. Those feelings are apt to convey a lower level of energy—one that is sluggish and reflects a lack of vigor and vivacity—to those around you. Regardless of any words you say to the contrary, we all pick up on one another's liveliness at all times. We get a feeling, or a sense about one another" and make assumptions about those around us based on what we sense.

Take stock of where you currently are with your wardrobe, your physicality, and the way you present yourself. Should you find that you may have let things go, there is no time like the present to get back on track. There is no need to wait for a New Year's resolution, or until after your vacation, or for when the holiday season has passed, or any other reason that might be keeping you stuck in undesirable circumstances. Vow to take action, to create and implement a plan to achieve the results you wish to have *now*.

Finally, picture how you practice self-care and dress for success around your loved ones at home. Do you take the same level of interest around those you see day in and day out as you do around those you see only occasionally? Think about how this outward expression of yourself sends unconscious messages to those closest to you and make adjustments accordingly as needed. Determine that you will demonstrate through your personal presentation to those closest to you that they are of great importance to you. *Magnificent!*

Notice what changes for you when you show up consistently in all aspects of your life with Every Feather in Place.

Worksheet Nine:
Every Feather in Place

It is time for an honest assessment: what does the outward reflection of your story say about you, in business and at home?

_____

_____

_____

_____

_____

Describe how engaged you are in the process of preparing yourself inside and out to put your best foot forward each day.

_____

_____

_____

_____

_____

How might others describe the level of care and concern you show for yourself?

_____

_____

_____

_____

_____

When do you notice you are less apt to put forth the extra effort with your clothing, appearance, and personal presentation?

_____

_____

_____

_____

_____

What messages do you believe you are conveying to others about you?

_____

_____

_____

_____

_____

Life Lesson Ten

Learn from Your Mistakes

Watch out! It is the hummingbird I have dubbed Rufous the Enforcer zooming in. He appears to be more concerned with guarding his feeder and chasing away unwanted visitors than stopping for nectar. In fact, the Rufous breed of hummingbird will ruthlessly defend his sources of nectar, attacking hummingbirds nearly double his size, and often defeating them in the process. Perhaps his quarrelsome behavior can be attributed to the fact that Rufous has the longest migration route of all hummingbirds, annually traveling thousands of miles round-trip from his winter home in Mexico to his summer breeding grounds in Montana while still others fly as far north and west as Alaska. I can only imagine the obstacles Rufous must overcome during his arduous migration each season. Like any weary traveler, is it any wonder he is cantankerous when he finally arrives?

Often, Rufous misses out on the sweetest nectar because he is too preoccupied with the chase to stop and appreciate the bounty right in front of him. He does not modify his behavior or learn from the error of his ways and so repeats this mistake time and time again.

Your life is one grand series of lessons on how to best be you. W hat do you believe you have discovered from your own life lessons so far? Perhaps as a result of some painful miscues in dealing with others, you have learned something about yourself and the way others see you. Do you find that you are now beginning to master the art of relationships and communication?

Have you learned the importance of conscious decision making, possibly as the outcome of a lesson that emerged from missing a great opportunity or neglecting to make a crucial decision? What do you see with respect to the consistency of your actions? As your habits either build you up or wear you down, what have you learned with regard to your habitual ways of being day in and day out? Perhaps you have arrived at a place in life where you desire to have a plan to fulfill your personal mission, whatever this may look like. How do you maintain and express constancy in your mission?

When it comes to learning from our mistakes, one school of thought tells us, "There are no mistakes in life, and everything happens for a reason." Whether you buy into that notion or not, there is a lot of value to be reaped from every mistake we make when we are able to connect it to a purpose. The question is "What can I learn from this?"

When we take a look at life from a broad perspective, we find that we do not always know what we want. When this is the case, our life lacks direction, we rarely act from a plan, and our life can meander its way to a place we never intended to be.

Picture for a moment a young couple planning their wedding with more care than they plan for their future life as man and wife. Without a clear idea of what they want or where their lives are headed, and not knowing how to say they do not know what they want, they begin plugging away without a plan, making all kinds of major decisions in the hasty blink of an eye. They may quickly have a couple of children, add a car payment or two and a mortgage that is too big for their combined income, and suddenly they wonder, "What happened to our marriage?"

Think for a moment about errors in judgment you have made in the past and where they led you to be in the present. You may have realized at the time that you were not making the right decision, or you may have learned it at some later point. Along the way on your journey, you had the opportunity to learn a thing or two. Whether or not you choose to learn and adapt based on this experience is up to you. Chances are that if you do not adapt in some way, you will have a similar experience somewhere down the road when you have long forgotten about this one. You will be presented with a new cast of characters who look a bit different, and you will therefore believe the situation *is* different. Then you will get that feeling—*Hmmm, this seems so familiar*—and eventually you will see it, and you will know: it happened again. You are being presented with the same lesson once more until you learn what you need to in order to progress, change, and make a different choice in the future.

Reflect now for a moment and consider what kinds of issues seem to reoccur in your life. Are you actively defining your path in life or going with the flow, wherever it might lead you, only to find it keeps leading you where you do not want to be? Do you find you are repeatedly involved in unhealthy or unsatisfactory relationships with partners or friends that frustrate you to no end?

When a client of mine is faced with a tough decision and is having difficulty sorting through it, I often ask them what their gut instinct is telling them to do. Although they will readily share what their intuition tells them, they will almost always follow it up by saying, "I am not sure that I should trust my intuition." When I ask them to recall a time when their instincts or intuition led them down the wrong path. Invariably, after some consideration while searching their memories, they come up empty. It is interesting to watch this scene unfold, as my question almost always jogs a memory that reminds my client of occasions when they went against a strong gut instinct—and paid a price. "Boy, I wish I had that decision back," they say, or "I should have listened to my intuition on that one!"

What can we take away from this? If we see ourselves sharing this same insight, we can choose to trust ourselves to tune in to our intuition, or gut instinct, and let it guide us to the right decision.

How in tune are you with your intuition? When you get a "feeling" that you should take a particular course of action but you do not know why, do you go with this instinct? Or do you ignore it and turn to your intellect to figure it out?

Consider for a moment how your intuition speaks to you. For some it speaks as a feeling that wells up in the pit of the stomach, or a sensation of butterflies in the chest. It may be just an inkling of "knowing" something without understanding how or why you know it. Many people experience powerful feelings of dread, a hit to the gut or sense of foreboding, when they intuit danger.

For me, intuition shows up in a combination of these ways. On a number of occasions I have had feelings of "knowing" something is the right choice for me. At other times I stop and think, *What is this red flag I am sensing here?* Sometimes I have gone with my intuition, and sometimes not. Generally, when I do, things manage to come together in the most unexpected and pleasing ways.

For instance, I do not know why prior to becoming a coach, with my experience and skill level after years in the travel and tourism industries, I chose to go with my gut and take an entry-level position with Carlson (formerly Carlson Companies, Carlson Cruises Worldwide) in its luxury cruise line division, RSSC (formerly Radisson Seven Seas Cruises, now Regent Seven Seas Cruises).

Within a few months, I was supervising a fantastic team of people in the Air/Sea Department, and a short time later managing the department before adding managerial responsibilities over the great team of people in the Operations Department, which was also in need of assistance at the time to help them grow. The six years I worked for that amazing company was one of the most rewarding and fruitful periods of professional growth I have ever enjoyed. Thank goodness I trusted my intuition, because intellectually, nothing about taking an entry-level job made sense on paper.

Intuition has also shown up for me in other ways. I recall a day in May many years ago when I was rafting lazily down the Yellowstone River with my friend Annette and her husband, Neil. The boat had a captain's chair in the middle with one set of oars and Neil was manning them. He was clowning around most of the afternoon, intentionally steering us into boulders that were sticking out above the swollen waters of the spring runoff so as to splash everyone on board. What might have been a welcome relief during the latter part of the summer when the sun was hot and the river was warm was not at all welcome on that particular afternoon in early May. The spring air temperature was in the high 60s and the water much, much colder than that. We were all shivering and wishing the float would soon end when we came to a large bend in the river.

As we began to round the bend, I experienced the most profound feeling: a sense of dread that made me feel intensely alert and very present in the moment. Looking ahead, I could only detect the same gorgeous expanse of river I had traveled for the past several miles. I wondered momentarily why on earth I had experienced that unsettling feeling—and then it happened.

Once again, Neil rowed us up against a large boulder jutting out above the surface of the river, although by now the inside of the boat had become wet and slippery from the water we had already taken on. This time, I went overboard, directly under the raft. The shock of the cold water overcame me as I sank deep into the river. I emerged quickly, coming up alongside the raft where my friends were able to grab hold of my arms. But the current was so strong that my legs were being pulled under the boat, making it difficult for me to hang on, hard for them to hold onto me, and impossible for me to climb back in. Through fast acting and fierce rowing, Neil swiftly maneuvered the raft onto a shoreline where I was able to gather myself up and get back aboard. That was my last rafting trip with Neil, and despite his many repeated attempts to get me to return on future outings, I politely declined.

The gravity of the gut hit I received shortly before that incident has remained with me for thirty years, and on one other occasion I experienced a reoccurrence of that same dreadful feeling. On the second occasion, I did not question the meaning of the message and instead reacted immediately to the feeling.

Late one afternoon a stranger appeared at the front door of my home posing a question that struck me as odd. Within an instant of opening the door, I again received an alarming sensation accompanied by feelings of foreboding. I felt the hair on the back of my neck stand up. Without another thought, I slammed the door and turned the deadbolt lock. The man stood there momentarily, staring at me through the locked door before turning to walk back to his vehicle. He sat in it there and watched me, and as I picked up the phone to call for assistance, he started the car and drove away.

Although this kind of situation had never happened to me before, the feeling was one I knew well, so I did not question the wisdom of my decision to quickly lock the door. I have no idea what his intention was, but my unequivocal sense was that nothing good would have come of leaving it open.

Recently I conducted a seminar for local area young professionals. One of the attendees, a young woman in the crowd, asked this question: "How do I know when I am receiving intuition and when it is just fear?"

How insightful of her! She recognized that intuition and fear are both internal messages, and wondered how to make a distinction between the two. The distinction I have experienced is that intuition is a feeling, a knowing, or a bodily sensation. Fear is generally perceived as a thought, therefore originating in the mind. When we are processing a fearful thought, it might take on a corresponding feeling of some kind, but it begins as a thought.

At times, as with my examples of the river and the stranger at my door, I perceived my intuition as "dread" or foreboding that may be labeled as fear. However, I was not thinking scary thoughts in those moments. My mind was open when I experienced those feelings.

Not recognizing the sensation the first time I experienced it, I had no frame of reference for it. The second time around, the sensation subconsciously triggered what I believe was my innate "fight or flight" response, causing me to react immediately. I did not stop to consider that it would be impolite to slam the door on the stranger—I simply acted on the feeling I was receiving.

More often than not, we tune out our intuition because our mind becomes involved and we cannot square our feelings with what we "think" we need to do. If we cannot figure it out by thinking, we decide our intuition must be wrong.

What is one of the most valuable lessons we can derive from our intuition as we learn from our mistakes? The more we tune in to our inner feelings and *sense of knowing,* the more we become aware of how useful intuition is in our lives. Pay close attention to the whispers of your heart, and see what follows when you are yielding to the guidance of that small, still voice inside you.

Worksheet Ten:
Learn From Your Mistakes

What patterns or similar experiences do you see reoccurring in
your life?

_____

_____

_____

_____

_____

How adept are you at tapping into your intuition?

_____

_____

_____

_____

_____

What signs or signals do you receive indicating your intuition is
communicating to you?

_____

_____

_____

_____

_____

When faced with facts and a contrary sense of intuition, which
would you defer to as a guide for your decision making?

_____

_____

_____

_____

_____

Life Lesson Eleven

Be Curious

*The most delightful broad-tailed hummingbird ever to visit
our home is the one I have nicknamed Lil Buddy. He appears
quite inquisitive, playful even, and he seems to enjoy getting
close to me. As I sit writing at the dining table on the south
deck, Lil Buddy flies under the table's umbrella directly toward me while descending to eye level, hovering mere inches
from my nose. While we observe one another, I wonder what
thoughts are running through his mind as he is suspended
there in stationary flight. Is he thinking,* When is she going
to refill the feeder on the south deck? *Or are his thoughts
much deeper than that:* If she is writing about me in that
hummingbird book of hers, I will give her something to
write about! *As quickly as he appeared, Lil Buddy darts off
toward the pines, making only the softest of sounds as he
goes; a gentle whir of his wings trails behind him and filters
through my consciousness.*

*C*uriosity may very well be the gateway to our intelligence. *When we embrace our curiosity, we become actively aware of our observations.* We begin to perceive everything, from the smallest details to the grand, glittery, and noteworthy red-carpet moments. The greater the range and depth of our curiosity, the more opportunities we have to experience what inspires and excites us. Curiosity, then, can be viewed as the stepping stone to many of life's most meaningful experiences, and when followed can lead us to pursue our passions, interests, and hobbies.

How curious are you? Do you observe and examine things closely, and then ask lots of great questions? How might you use your curiosity as a springboard to further your understanding of those around you?

Think for a moment about some of the people you most enjoy having a conversation with. They may be friends, family, or acquaintances. Perhaps they are people you know in the working world. What attributes do they have that draw you in? What makes them interesting to be around, and what do you suppose makes someone a great conversationalist? If you are thinking that great conversationalists are as interested as they are interesting, you already know what they do differently from most. They listen. They are curious about other people and they ask questions, both to build rapport and to learn something new.

One of the most important skills we can cultivate as part of our personal development is that of listening. Listening is often taken for granted, since most of us equate becoming a *better speaker* with becoming a *better communicator*. What, then, about our ability to listen effectively?

There are three ways of listening we will explore in this chapter which I have further adapted from the iPEC coach training program. See if you can notice the type of listening you most often use in your daily life.

Listening to Respond

This form of listening is superficial and does nothing to enhance understanding or build rapport between the speaker and the listener. The listener is considering their own agenda and is not fully engaged with the speaker while they wait to respond. This listening is rarely gratifying to the speaker, as the listener is focused on their own needs and agenda. The listener may be lost in thought as the speaker is communicating, or distracted in some other way such as multitasking, their attention split. The listener often responds in "tell mode" at this listening level, and is quick to provide an answer or a solution based on their personal frame of reference and experience. For example, here is a conversation that might take place when one coworker shares her feelings with a colleague:

"This has been a tough day. I just had an awful account review with Meg. She kept speaking over me, and cutting me off every time I tried to explain myself to her."

Her coworker who was *listening to respond* quickly shoots back, "You should get your ducks in a row before talking to Meg about accounts."

Consider how you might feel receiving a response like this if you were the speaker. You can see why it is regarded as superficial listening, and may be best used to exchange relatively benign information, such as acknowledging someone you pass in the hallway. It is a courtesy check-in more than anything else. It is not going to build rapport or enhance a relationship for you, and while that may be fine in certain circumstances, be aware that this is a relatively ineffective level of listening.

Listening to Hear

This form is more engaging: the listener hears the speaker's words and focuses on what is being said. Although this is a deeper level of listening than listening to respond, the listener will still miss much of the message that is being communicated, focusing on the words and not the intent behind them. The listener often responds in "tell mode" here too, although now the listener applies logic in a response directed to the speaker's perspective. Here is how the coworkers' conversation might go with *listening to hear:*

> "This has been a tough day. I just had an awful account review with Meg. She kept speaking over me, and cutting me off every time I tried to explain myself to her."

> "It does sound like you've had a tough day. Thank goodness you can put that review behind you now, and move on."

This way of listening helps us ascertain information as we focus on comprehending at a deeper level. As another example, picture yourself listening to someone give you directions. You are attentive while applying logic and reasoning in order to comprehend what you hear.

Listening to Understand

This is deep listening, most beneficial for building stronger relationships and a greater appreciation of others. The listener is fully tuned in to the speaker. They hear the words that are being spoken and also pay attention to what is *not* being said. That is, they focus on the speaker without distraction and pick up nonverbal clues too. Through this engaged form of listening, we are able to grasp the speaker's energy and emotion. We notice whether they are nervous, upset, excited, distracted, happy, or overwhelmed. The listener often responds to the speaker in a way that expresses this understanding, moving from the "tell mode" to the "ask mode" as a way to gain further understanding. Notice how the conversation shifts:

"This has been a tough day. I just had an awful account review with Meg. She kept speaking over me, and cutting me off every time I tried to explain myself to her."

"I hear what you are saying, and I am picking up on your nervousness as you are speaking. Is there something more going on with you and Meg that you would like to share with me so I can better understand where you are coming from?"

Listening to understand is the most powerful form because we are gathering the intent and the emotion behind the spoken words. We learn much more about what is going on with someone when we use this form of listening—and, *it is important to take into account that people will not always say what they mean.* When we listen to the words alone, we miss a large part of the message. In order to pick up on nonverbal clues and underlying messages—as happens when the words and body language or expressions are incongruent—we must pay full attention. We naturally tend to disregard the words, and favor the nonverbal clues when there is discrepancy between the two. Picture the friend who says, "I am telling you, everything is just *fine!*" What do you believe? Do the words or the emotional emphasis on "*fine!*"carry the most meaning?

When people are listened to in this manner, they feel deeply valued and validated. They view the listener differently too. It is such a rarity in our hurry-up society to slow down and pay attention to one another that this simple act of listening to understand towers head and shoulders above our typical interactions. A listener who practices this level of listening is viewed by the speaker as someone who genuinely cares.

Let's further explore how these ways of listening appear in our daily life.

Unfortunately, most of us spend the greatest portion of our time listening to respond. In the work environment, we may be immersed in the computer, talking on the phone, or texting while someone asks us a question. Rarely do we look up or narrow our focus to engage listening at a higher level. We miss opportunities to make deeper connections with those around us, and at the same time we risk missing an important part of the message.

Have you ever had the experience of having an entire conversation with someone who then took action on that conversation—but not in the way you intended?

"When I asked about it, you told me you wanted the project handled this way," they say.

You reluctantly admit, "But that's not what I meant. I guess I should have paid closer attention when you were speaking to me."

How might things have gone differently? If we had been fully engaged in the conversation with this person rather than giving it only partial attention, chances are we would have recognized a lack of understanding and worked through it at that time.

Have you had a similar experience with a customer or a client, where expectations were not met due to poor listening?

"That's not what I ordered," they say.

"But I thought that was what you said you wanted," you respond.

Where did the breakdown in listening occur?

Now it should be said that we also regularly engage in this lowest form of listening at home with those closest to us. Picture a child trying to communicate with his or her parents as they are running through the "to do" list, perusing social media, talking on the phone, sorting laundry, or engaged in any number of other daily domestic activities. Even young children can sense when they do not have our full attention. Tugging on a parent's sleeve, the child says, "Watch me! Look at me." Our five-year-old grandson has been known to place his hands gently on either side of an adult family member's face and turn their head to face him when he wants to ensure they are listening to him. He makes a powerful point.

How much effort does it take for your family members to garner your full listening attention? Hopefully they do not have to adopt our grandson's technique in order to be heard. It's funny that we take communication with our nearest and dearest so lightly, isn't it? The good news is that once we are aware that we are accustomed to doing this, we can modify our behavior. Imagine the strides you will make in your relationships simply by becoming a better listener. Now *that* is inspiring!

What are the keys to developing the habits of listening to understand? There are a few simple steps that will help you build the right framework to become more receptive in your listening. This is not groundbreaking territory, and you will likely find this information is simply a review for you. If you find that you are already regularly listening at the deepest level, good for you—and for those around you! If instead you recognize that you have regularly been listening at the lower levels of engagement, and you find that your communications with others are not scratching the surface of their fullest potential, that is fine too. You recognize that you have room for improvement, and this list is also for you!

- Clear your thoughts and prepare to pay attention.
- Focus on the speaker while holding no agenda of your own.
- Turn toward the speaker, being mindful of your body language (arms crossed do not communicate openness; sitting forward in your chair indicates attentiveness).
- Ignore distractions giving the speaker your undivided attention.
- Pay close attention to the nonverbal clues coming from the speaker.
- Listen and observe to engage fully without dropping to the lower levels of listening.
- Maintain eye contact and communicate understanding with a nod, smile, or other gesture that is appropriate to the message being conveyed.
- Ask clarifying questions, and provide feedback on what you comprehend to be the speaker's message to insure you are on the same page.

You might find it useful to run through this list from time to time before you meet with another person until the process becomes second nature for you. As you become a more attentive listener, you might also begin to listen for the speaker's *intent*. The intent is the "driver" or the "motivator" behind the words. *When listening for intent, notice words that are powerful and show a willingness to take action.* A speaker who is fully committed to action will use words such as *I choose, I want, I desire.* Conversely, words that indicate low commitment are words like *I can't, I won't, I must, I have to,* and *I need to.*

Picture two people having this conversation:

"I have to start a diet."
"I know. I need to lose weight too."

The words "have" and "need" indicate that although both people see the benefits they would like to receive from taking action, they are not fully in the mind-set to energetically move forward on the task. It is possible for them to get under way with their weight-loss intention, but unless they *choose* to commit at a higher level, the desired outcome will fall by the wayside more often than not.

When we approach life regularly *listening to understand*, we work from the assumption that there is always more to learn from those around us. Adopting this outlook in our conversations enhances our potential for growth and builds strength in our relationships as we table our own thoughts and opinions to fully listen. Listening with this level of curiosity, we gain knowledge and experience through our sense of wonder and open-mindedness, like the hummingbird.

Worksheet Eleven:
Be Curious

In what situations do you most often find yourself listening to respond?

_____
_____
_____
_____
_____

When do you engage in listening to hear?

_____
_____
_____
_____
_____

In what interactions do you see yourself regularly listening
to understand?

_____

_____

_____

_____

_____

Which of your key relationships would benefit most if you engage
at the highest level of listening to understand?

_____

_____

_____

_____

_____

Life Lesson Twelve

Make Course Corrections

The energetic hummingbird is often referred to as the avian helicopter, highly maneuverable and flying in a fashion unlike any other bird. While most birds appear to require planning as they descend from a point in the sky to a landing place on solid ground, a hummingbird can hover in mid-flight, back up, move forward, or fly side to side, instantaneously and energetically. Generally a bird's wings flap up and down when it takes off and lands with a typical straight in, vertical pattern, but the hummingbird wing action uniquely flutters back and forth in an elegant figure eight. This wing movement creates tremendous lift and thrust, allowing for flight in any direction. Whether maneuvering backward or upside down, the agile hummingbird makes course corrections as needed to remain right where he wishes to be at all times.

If you do not change direction, you may end up where you are heading.
—Lao Tzu

*L*ife is too short for us to be able to experience everything firsthand. Luckily, we share the world with a host of interesting companions, loved ones, and strangers who also have much wisdom to impart to us. Their journeys and experiences enrich and enhance our own.

Even through experiences that are most challenging, we stand to learn a lot, perhaps because they are so challenging. There is a subtle give and take between ourselves and those around us as we teach each other and learn together. Sometimes the lesson is as valuable when we learn "how not to be" as is learning from a mentor "what positive possibilities will be."

If I am walking with two other men, each of them will serve as my teacher. I will pick out the good points of the one and imitate them, and the bad points of the other and correct them in myself.
—Confucius

When you feel like you are stuck in a pattern that is not serving you, give rise to your own maneuverability, like that of the hummingbird, and make a course correction. You can do this at any time you choose. The first step in making any sort of correction or change is always the *awareness* that change is needed.

If you have awareness, you can recognize, for instance, that you have surrounded yourself with people who are largely negative, complaining, and prone to look at the short side of life, and it is probably draining your energy. Notice how their negativity affects you. Do you see a change in your outlook on life? How different is your frame of mind when you are surrounded with negativity? Are you experiencing turmoil in your work and in your personal relationships? How might the negativity of those around you be affecting your own state of well-being?

As a department manager for Carlson Companies, I was in a position to hire and train a number of employees over the years. The majority quickly showed themselves to be positive, hard-working, self-motivated, and highly engaged in the workplace. They were a delight to work with. There were also a few who showed themselves quite the opposite. They were negative, actively seeking conflict with coworkers and clients, disengaged in the work environment, and largely unmotivated. These employees were a drain on resources and on the energy of everyone around them.

I learned that when most qualifications were equal, I should hire first for integrity and character and second for sparkle and enthusiasm. I could always teach job skills, but internal traits like integrity, character, and attitude were not learned behaviors.

It was often challenging to find a new employee with the right stuff. Those who interviewed the best generally had the most interview practice. That is not necessarily a good thing. They may have been out in the job market for a while, or in some cases were continually "liberated" to re-enter the job market!

I determined it best to trust what my gut told me. If "something just doesn't seem right about this candidate" or "I am not sure I've received full disclosure from that candidate," my gut was usually right.

What I found most interesting took place after I had inadvertently chosen a negative employee to join the team. Within a day or two of coming on board and being introduced to all of the other employees, they would naturally gravitate to employees from other departments who were actively being disciplined by their supervisors. In short, the negative employees would draw together, energy attracting like energy, as the story goes, and I would think, *man, I did not see that one coming!* Likewise, the positive employees who became welcome additions to the department, true to their cheerful natures, would find camaraderie with the other shining stars in their midst.

If you want to thrive in life and not just survive, you have to recognize when it is time for a course correction—and then make it! Should you find that you are ready to initiate some important changes in your life and your relationships, but you feel some resistance to implementing a change, the following series of questions should help you sort through it. Once you find the underlying issue, you can tackle it head-on! Ready? Great! Take into account the following questions:

What is the challenge of my current situation?

What do I *gain or accept* by maintaining my current situation?

What do I *surrender or forgo* by maintaining my current situation?

What change am I considering?

What stands to improve in my life with this change?

What am I willing to commit to for this change to occur?

Ask yourself point-blank, *What is going on with me that makes these the people I continue to surround myself with?* Your capacity to see the part that you are playing in the drama that unfolds around you will help you recognize that your ability to make a course correction is a simple matter of exercising your own free will. *Good for you!*

Think about what it takes to overcome the pattern of involving yourself with the unconstructive walk of life once and for all so you can move on. This does not pertain solely to the workplace; remember to review conditions and relationships in your personal life as well.

What do you observe about others when they interact with those closest to them? Have you ever noticed people talking to their spouses and other family members in ways that show disrespect and disregard for their feelings: raised voices, hurtful labels? Maybe they hung up the phone or walked away from a conversation, muttering with disgust and disparaging those they "loved" behind their backs. Often those same individuals have a habit of "joking" about the "crazy family member" or "the rotten kid." Although this language is generally intended to be funny, or to build rapport with whoever else may be nearby, these actions and words shed light on the person speaking them. *What people say about others says mountains about themselves.*

Watch the signs and signals that you pick up from others early on, when you are first getting to know them. Although anyone may have an "off" day, people do not suddenly "turn negative" one day. *We each have an overall state of mind that is either positive or negative, and we demonstrate it early and often in the ways we speak, think, and act.* It is then up to you, once you recognize negative behavior, to do what you need to do to distance yourself from it and those who are perpetuating it.

It may be useful to reflect upon the notion that if people talk to you about others, they will also talk to others about you. Choose your friends wisely taking precautions against being impressed upon in any undesirable or uninspiring way. Words intended to belittle, disparage, or tear apart another individual reflect a lesser evolved way of being, and that's not who you are at your core!

A man's growth is seen in the successive choirs of his friends.
—Ralph Waldo Emerson

Instead of connecting with the people who view life as one big bummer, consciously choose to be in the company of the people you respect, admire, and can learn the most from. They will help you grow in ways that will enrich the lives of those around you rather than detract from them. As you grow, you cannot help but add depth and meaning to our own life. Now see yourself creating a ripple effect, sending waves of positivity out into the world, impacting countless lives for years to come. That is the power you have to impact others, positively or negatively. Never take that power lightly.

Is it time to shake up your habitual routines and make some fresh changes in your life? How will it feel to shed those negative hangers-on like the bad habit they have become? Happily bid the "negatives" a fond farewell as you make your course correction in a highly positive and productive way.

Worksheet Twelve:
Make Course Corrections

How do you demonstrate a positive attitude through your
thoughts, words, and deeds?

_____

_____

_____

_____

_____

What if any differences do you see in your commitment to being
positive at home, at work, or in your community?

_____

_____

_____

_____

_____

What drains on your energy are you tolerating in your life right
now? (negative people, disorganization, lack of support
systems, clutter …)

_____

_____

_____

_____

_____

What would it take to deal with this energy drain once and for all
rather than continue to cope with it?

_____

_____

_____

_____

_____

Life Lesson Thirteen

Vocalize Your Desires

The scent of the river rises and drifts lazily through the house on a radiant summer morning. I love the way my senses are slowly brought to life each day. As I open my eyes, the mountains, river, and forest provide a visual feast while the air smells so sweet and clean that I pinch myself to make sure I am not in some beautiful dream state. The sounds of the forest seem content to whisper...but wait! What was that? A high-pitched squeaking—chit a chitit—emanating simultaneously from multiple hummingbirds reverberates through the screen door. So much for my Zen moment—now I am fully awake. The whistling, popping vocalization rings out in earnest as one hummingbird arrives at the back feeder only to find other birds already comfortably perched and feeding there. The newcomer displays, zipping speedily back and forth near the feeder, while the others quickly take their leave, allowing the more vocal bird to have his seat at the table. He fluffs his wings, puffs his tiny chest, and settles in to drink his morning nectar. Message delivered, and clearly received!

*W*hat sort of communicator are you? Do you clearly and succinctly articulate your message and then check for understanding to ensure your message was received and interpreted the way it was intended? If you do, you should know that you have a better than average ability to communicate and create understanding in your relationships. The quality of your relationships is largely the result of the communication style you regularly employ with others.

Communication takes place any time two or more people exchange information or ideas. The fact that communication has taken place does not guarantee that it was effective, however. If the receiver did not interpret the message the way the sender intended, communication was a "miss" and not a "hit." At times, wordiness can cloud the message and cause confusion in the listener. To be most effective, you should first plan what you want to say and then say it in as few words as possible without leaving out any important details. Effective communication can be defined simply as the message sent being received and interpreted in the manner in which it was intended.

Be on the lookout for the common symptoms of poor communication. They often include conflict, stress, uncertainty, mismatched expectations, and anger. Emotion is the red flag that tells us something has gone awry with our communication.

If you notice that you frequently have trouble getting your point across, ask yourself the following questions:

What might be missing from my messages that lead to frustration or misunderstanding?

Is it my choice of words? Are there too many or too few details to create understanding?

Is the focus of my communication clear and concise?

How is the message delivered?

If the people with whom I have had difficulty communicating were here, how might they describe the way I communicate?

How differently might people respond to me if I were to try another approach?

What might a new approach in my communication look like?

When you create a habit of checking for understanding when communicating with others, you offer them the opportunity to seek clarification. As the effectiveness of your communication increases as a result of this practice, note the positive changes that result.

Next, consider how your language or vocabulary affects your ability to communicate. A few years ago I was attending a staff meeting along with other department managers and supervisors. I was listening to the team communicate around the boardroom table, and noting how much informal language and slang had crept into our place of business over a period of time. Although expressions such as "my bad" used in lieu of "my mistake" might be acceptable in some personal conversations, it does nothing to build or enhance your credibility as a professional.

Realize that words matter. Through the use of good vocabulary, you demonstrate your understanding of what it takes to be successful in the work environment. Put aside language that is best used in informal social settings in favor of more professional language to improve your professional profile.

Another simple and seemingly benign act for many women is the overuse of apology. "I'm sorry" is all too common language for some. It is used as a regular response in a variety of situations:

- When a mistake is brought to their attention—"I'm so sorry. That won't happen again"
- When speaking up, as when drawing attention to the boss who moved on in his presentation before you were ready— "I'm sorry. Would you please go back? You changed the slide before I took down the information."

- When disagreeing with a colleague—"I'm sorry, I disagree with you."

I wonder why we are so sorry. None of these examples are likely to require an apology, so what is really going on here?

Many women are accustomed to apologizing as a way to maintain a calm environment, and they use the words "I'm sorry" to defuse conflict. From another viewpoint, the regular use of apologies is often perceived as lack of confidence or low self-esteem. That may very well be the case with someone who will quickly give up their position in a discussion by apologizing. If that is not your intent, consider language that acknowledges the other person or the situation but not at the cost of your self-esteem.

In the examples above, how different might you feel if you shared the following responses instead of "I'm sorry"?

- "Thank you for bringing that mistake to my attention, so I can ensure it does not happen in the future."
- "That last slide covered some excellent points. Would you please expand on that while I jot down some additional notes?"
- "We view that issue differently. Let's see if together we can find some common ground."

Another way you can vocalize your desires is to address what isn't working and see how it might be improved when you speak up.

There are times in all of our lives when things seem so easy breezy, like a gentle Chinook wind over the summer plains. Life runs rather effortlessly and we happily go with the flow during those times. Does "easy breezy" currently describe your own life? At other times, life more closely resembles hurricane force winds than the tranquil Chinook variety, right?

I am fortunate to be able to interact with a lot of fantastic people through my coaching practice, and I have found that there is always something profound going on with everyone I meet. Oftentimes, looks are deceiving, and that something profound is just below the surface for most people. We all carry a lot around on our shoulders, worrying about what will be, stressing over what was done or said, or should have been done or said, and so on. More often than not, people share with me their fear of being helpless to change the situation they find themselves in. They have tried to find solutions in the past, and eventually, when those failed, they threw in the towel.

Assuming because we tried something in the past that didn't work then, it won't work now, keeps us stuck in our current reality. To move forward doing good work, having great relationships, and being at our personal best, we must choose to speak up and surface the things that are not working in our lives so we may learn and grow through them. Otherwise, those issues hang around us like a ball and chain we drag to and fro everywhere we go. *When we choose not to address issues, those issues cast a shadow over us, affecting everything we do and everyone we come into contact with.*

Have you ever had the occasion to observe someone who was in a place of challenge but was unwilling to do anything different to improve their situation? Maybe this question is closer to home, and you recognize something in yourself that is keeping you stuck where you do not wish to be.

Over the years I have encountered countless employees struggling with relationships in the workplace. Disagreements in personality and work style among coworkers can be enough to turn the average workplace upside down. For example, when highly social employees are paired with or stationed near more introverted, quiet employees, tempers can flare. The introvert quickly tires of the talkative, social colleague, while the extrovert wants a colleague who is more engaging than the introvert he finds himself stuck with.

There are also employees who find fault with everything from their fellow staff members to the company's policies, and on and on the list goes. Their negativity can cause angst and stress for those around them. Or how about jealousy in the workplace, when some employees are just certain that others are receiving preferential treatment or are paid more but carry less of a load?

As a manager when communication became strained between team members in our departments, I was a fan of the concept of cross-training. Boy, there was nothing like walking in another's shoes to gain an appreciation of the challenges they faced on a daily basis. In my experience, it was a lack of such an understanding that often created an environment of interpretations. *When we don't know what is going on with another person, we fill in the blanks based on our limited exposure to who they are and what we think we know.*

Generally, a little time spent cross-training or job sharing could clear up that problem. Immersion in another person's day-to-day world, the challenges they face, and the obstacles they overcome is often just the eye-opener needed to bring about cooperation and understanding.

There will be times when no matter what you do, others will not be happy. Some people go through life assuming the worst. They look for ways to reinforce their belief that they are being treated unfairly. Through their constant search to find fault or identify problems with others, they draw conflict to themselves, thus reinforcing their belief that they are right. Until they are ready to accept the role they play in creating the conflict they are caught in, there is little that can be done to change the situation.

When work struggles involve an employee and their boss—as is the case with the micromanager or the overbearing, condescending boss—the employee often feels powerless to effect change. This person is pretty easy to recognize. They appear resigned, browbeaten, even defeated. They become paralyzed and believe that any attempt on their part to rectify the situation would lead to a blackballing, discipline, or possibly firing. It is understandable and completely natural to feel discouraged if you feel singled out or mistreated by your boss.

Decide, however, that something in this experience is giving you an opportunity to evolve in some way. You may not know what this opportunity is in the moment, but down the road you will likely come to see how a period of challenge has provided some benefits to you.

I have never subscribed to the notion that we are powerless. We are all making choices at all times. That is our right, our privilege, and our "response-ability." Response-ability is nothing more than our ability to thoughtfully choose a response rather than succumb to a thoughtless knee-jerk reaction.

Consider the options you might have. Would a private conversation with your boss allow you to find a greater understanding of how you might better work together? What, if anything, might you be doing to contribute to or compound the issues as you see them? How might you articulate how the environment is affecting your ability to be productive and do your job?

What if the boss has no idea that the way they manage affects those around them? How might your speaking up actually offer an opportunity for the boss to see things from another perspective?

Successful people stand up to what is not working in their lives even when it is very hard to do so. Granted, not every challenge we meet can be changed, but nothing can ever be changed until it is addressed.

It is natural to feel some hesitation and resistance to having a tough conversation with someone, regardless of whether they are your boss, a colleague, a friend, or a family member. When we choose to ignore what is not working in our lives, rarely do things improve on their own; rather, what we resist persists. Speak up about what isn't working and take the opportunity to explore, advance, and improve all that you can.

What do you stand to gain as you vocalize your desires?

Worksheet Thirteen:
Vocalize Your Desires

Take stock of the language you use on a regular basis. What slang or casual language do you hear yourself and those in your interpersonal circle using?

_____

_____

_____

_____

_____

Where do you have room to improve your communication?

_____

_____

_____

_____

_____

What issues have you been putting up with? What coping strategies
have you been using to live with the situation?

_____

_____

_____

_____

_____

What would it take to overcome those issues once and for all?

_____

_____

_____

_____

_____

What will you commit to doing this week to take action to become
a better listener?

_____

_____

_____

_____

_____

How will you measure your success at becoming a better listener?

_____

_____

_____

_____

_____

Life Lesson Fourteen

Fly Higher

Most hummingbirds seem uninterested as other birds sidle up next to them at the feeder or settle in nearby to pollinate a large blooming plant. This is not the case with feisty Rufous the Enforcer. He appears to be more obsessed with chasing other birds away than actually doing the work he is there to do—drink nectar! Despite the fact that he is one of the smallest birds on the planet, he will not hesitate to attack crows, hawks, or jays that infringe on his territory. Rufous will spend much of his time and energy making a fuss, displaying dramatic territorial behavior and fighting against others. This quarrelsome aspect of the hummer's personality may be reflected in some human behaviors as well.

When you think about *attitude,* what comes to mind? Do you find yourself running through a list of those you know and how their attitudes affect you at home and work? Perhaps you recall your own attitude and reflect on how it may propel you forward—or at times hold you back. While some people appear happy and easy to get along with, others seem to struggle with just about everybody they meet. What makes up our attitude anyway?

Simply put, our attitude is our disposition, inclination, or natural emotional outlook. The way we express what is going on inside our minds and our hearts is revealed through our attitude.

When we have a healthy view of our own self-worth, an overall agreeable temperament, and a favorable outlook on life, we project a positive attitude. From a positive perspective, we also view those around us in a favorable light and focus on acknowledging the good in them. In the face of difficult experiences, a positive viewpoint enables us to see challenges, stresses, and strains as natural parts of life. It provides the energy necessary for us to continue moving forward each day. With such a disposition and an agreeable mind-set, we do not allow obstacles to put a halt to our success. Life's stumbling blocks become stepping stones, and the walls that appear to hinder our progress are transformed into hurdles we can learn to clear. Our affable attitude helps bolster our energy enough to create solutions, allowing us to lead productive lives despite the circumstances we may face.

As a positive person myself, I have heard on a number of occasions over the years, *"Get your head out of the clouds and come down to earth with the rest of us realists!"* It might be a common misconception that positive people are out of touch with the realities of life, yet all of the positive people I know are well versed in the issues facing our society and the world at large. The fact that they do not choose to hammer away at discussions about the day's headlines generally has little to do with lack of understanding or denial of the issues; rather, they realize that when they are powerless to positively impact the outcomes of those situations, it serves no one to belabor the issues. Since we have only so much energy to spend in a day, we get to choose whether we want to spend it arguing, worrying, and fretting, or shift our focus in a new direction where we can do some good.

How much bad news is *enough already?* When we consider the nature of the stories that sell newspapers in our country, our politics, reality TV, and all of the other ways negativity streams into our homes and lives each day, is it any wonder that we become stressed?

Recently while conducting a seminar with a group of women, I asked for a show of hands for how many watched the nightly news. As hands went up, I asked if any noticed that most nightly news programs ran about twenty minutes of bad news and wrapped up with a two-minute happy segment or inspirational story. A collective groan from the audience registered their recognition and distaste, although we all seemed to agree this was the networks' attempt to leave us on a high note, faint though it may be.

How different might our society be if the news were delivered in reverse? What if we had twenty minutes of uplifting and inspiring human-interest stories, and somewhere in the mix a two-minute segment of "other" news: *Hey, consumers, it's dangerous to deep fry a frozen turkey* or *Be careful, America, it is risky to travel around the middle east.* I wonder how our society would function if our current reality were turned upside down in that way. How might all of the good news stories being repeated by millions of people around the dinner table each evening, at the coffeemaker at work each morning, and with neighbors across the fence each afternoon change our reality? How can we make that happen? *Is there a network executive somewhere who would be so bold as to start GNN—Good News Network?*

What if we all spend our time seeking ways to inspire and uplift others in every way we can rather than participating in discussions about the negative events and circumstances around us? Are you with me? Right on! No more grumbling and complaining. *Life is hard. Work stinks. What in the world is our country coming to? Did you hear the terrible news today?*

I find that my life works better when I take a positive approach and maintain a good attitude. With full awareness that I get to choose what I allow into my experience, *I see myself as an enthusiastic gardener, forever cultivating what I want to have blossom in my life, harvesting my time and energy like precious, limited natural resources.* I guard my good attitude by limiting my exposure to outside negative influences the way a gardener protects her flowers from harmful invasive species that, left unattended, will spread to overtake the good. This means I choose to forgo scandalous reality TV shows, 24/7 news broadcasts, and gossipy tabloids that fill the newsstand at the grocery checkout. Although on occasion I have been known to read a thrilling novel or watch a scary movie, in general, I prefer to spend my time reading inspirational books and watching educational programs or comedies. *Ellen* (DeGeneres) is a TV program I enjoy. Her warm, inspiring nature gladdens the heart, and since Ellen is also a comedian, it is possible to both laugh and cry during a typical episode of her show. Heck, it just feels good to tune in! I also spend time nurturing a positive attitude by appreciating nature, listening to music, exercising, and using my creative energy to cook and write. These activities lift me up instead of wearing me down and provide an outlet to help me maintain a sunny disposition even in the most trying times.

What gets in the way of a positive attitude? Negative thinking, right? Since we already accept that we are in charge of the thoughts we think, with some practice we can learn to be aware of the negativity flowing in and discover ways to manage it. The challenge is that a detrimental mind-set is not always easy to recognize. For example, when we repeatedly suspend our happiness until something else is accomplished, or acquired we subject ourselves to a sneaky, subtle form of negativity. When allowed to continue unchecked, this insidious thought process undermines our self-esteem. Similar to the confidence draining message, *I am not enough*, reviewed in Lesson One the underlying message here is *I don't have enough.*

Let's zoom in and take a closer look. *What does it mean to suspend happiness?* See if you can relate to any of the following statements:

> I will be happy when I get a decent job.
> I will be happy when I finally receive that promotion.
> I will be happy when I meet a nice guy.
> I will be happy when I can travel more.
> I will be happy when I have recognition for all my hard work.
> I will be happy when people treat me with respect.
> I will be happy when I can afford a new car.
> I will be happy when I lose thirty pounds.
> I will be happy when the kids go off to college.
> I will be happy when I can pay off my debts.
> I will be happy when this project is complete.
> I will be happy when I retire.

We may not view this form of thinking as outright negativity because we are not having contrary thoughts like *I hate being thirty pounds overweight. I don't like my job. I can't meet a good guy.* Nevertheless, do you sense the power the words have to diminish your self-esteem by creating a belief that you *don't have enough*, and you are *never quite there*?

If you find that any of these thoughts resonate with you, you can be sure some very cunning negative thinking has wriggled into your mind. This thought process comes from feelings of lack, when we view life as not good enough, because we don't have enough, and surely the next thing on our list will make us happy once we have it! Right? In reality, the chances are once we have acquired the current items on our list, a new list will already be in place. *I will be happy when I have new clothes that better fit since I lost the weight. I will be happy when others begin to acknowledge my weight loss.* On, and on it goes. These thoughts of lack erode a positive attitude by keeping us focused on what we think we are missing.

Choose to be happy at this moment instead. There is no need to delay thinking positively or feeling good about your life. You are not what you have, nor what you do—so decide to feel good now with the understanding that the energy you radiate into the world shimmers and shines back on you. If you wish to be happy, just determine that you will—and there you will find yourself.

Attitude is not the be-all and end-all. It has nothing to do with ability and everything to do with the way in which we go about doing what we do.

When pressure is applied, and we are under stress or strain, our fears and insecurities are revealed through our actions.

If our attitudes are on balance negative, we tend to view challenges and anyone associated with them as "the problem." We work in conflict mode against others and we aggressively pursue our own interests through anger, manipulation, force, coercion, or whatever means we believe will get us the result we desire.

It is true that if you are talented and possess great skills, a strong education, and a bad attitude, you may do well enough in life. You may find a way to make a comfortable living, reach your goals, and achieve what you set out to do. Along the way, however, harboring a bad attitude will color your world by adding challenges to your every turn. Regardless of your talents, skills, and abilities, you will not get along well with other people and they in turn will not support you. People want to be associated with those they like and can get along with. Without their support, you may still be able to create a measure of success for yourself, but to what extent will your attitude and the way others respond to it affect your *quality of life?*

Over the years I have watched a number of talented people work their way out of good companies and lose significant opportunities all because they had the wrong attitudes. Bad attitudes can manifest in a number of different ways. Some people are outwardly hostile and aggressive, snapping and sneering at anyone and everyone near them. We all know to *stay away from Mary when she is having a bad day.* Others are more covert in their bad attitudes. They may get along well enough with others so as not to draw any attention to themselves while undermining or usurping relationships and authority at every opportunity. They will never miss a chance to badmouth the company, the boss, their coworkers; even their family members and spouse are not above being targeted. Everyone *else* is the problem.

Regardless of the way a bad attitude shows up at work, it is vital to the morale and success of the company that it be nipped in the bud. Allowed to go unchecked, a single bad attitude will cost a company a great deal in time and resources, not to mention clients and high-quality employees who will not tolerate a hostile work environment.

In a family, a bad attitude can be contagious, especially when it comes from someone viewed as a leader. If you have ever been in the company of a family that suffered groupthink and shared a bad attitude, you recognize it in the general outlook they have on life, the government, the economy, and everyone around them. What a disservice they do to each other when they allow negativity to permeate them so thoroughly. This attitude creates a foundation for narrowmindedness, intolerance, and prejudice.

Attitude might not make a difference if we lived alone on an island. We could carry on in any way we wanted with utter disregard for the outcome of our words and actions. The reality is that we require other people's support as colleagues, contemporaries, customers, or friends. And they require our support.

A positive attitude transforms problems into possibilities. *In a negative environment, the positive attitude is the proverbial buoyancy device that keeps others afloat.* It can become the lifeline, producing much needed levity in otherwise heavy situations. With a lightness of mind, people are able to function at a higher level and thus maintain their productivity.

In my experience, regardless of whether an individual is primarily negative or positive, when they find themselves going through a rough patch but hold out hope that it will improve, they gravitate toward highly energetic, positive people. It is as if there is an innate understanding within each of us that the world's problems are only solved through the most positive solutions. It is when people lose hope and feel helpless that they remain stuck in negative thinking patterns and bad attitudes. Before attempting to judge another human being based on their attitude, consider that you might be dealing with someone who feels they have no hope. With that thought in mind, what might change for you in the way you view such a person and extend yourself to them?

When we look beyond simple personality styles, even those adults with a high degree of likability and an affable personality may not "gel" well with others from time to time. Even the most positive among us may battle an occasional bad attitude. The difference is when the attitude becomes pervasive and clouds our everyday thinking.

The most important lesson about attitude is this: it is a choice! During each moment, we get to choose who we are and how we show up in our lives. Do we choose to go through life giving everyone and everything the best we have to offer, or do we wish to moan, and groan our way through it?

The world stands to benefit enormously from the excellence you have to offer. Imagine the sense of satisfaction you will gain by showing up every day giving life your all, and in the process inspiring those around you to give their all. Are you beginning to sense the impact your attitude has on others? Feeling motivated? Good! Go ahead, give life your best, and rest knowing that will *always* be enough.

What do you envision your life to be as you Fly Higher?

Worksheet Fourteen:
Fly Higher

What is your overall outlook and attitude about life?

_____
_____
_____
_____
_____

On a scale of 1 to 10, what is your current satisfaction level with
your attitude?

_____
_____
_____
_____
_____

What would it take for you to reach a 9 or 10?

_____

_____

_____

_____

_____

What beliefs do you hold about your attitude and the attitudes of those around you? (For example, *It's impossible to be positive when surrounded by negative people.*)

_____

_____

_____

_____

_____

When you choose to do so, how do you shift your attitude from negative to positive?

_____

_____

_____

_____

_____

Life Lesson Fifteen

Gratitude Naturally

It is a picture-perfect summer morning in the Flathead Valley. The sun beams brilliantly as it crests the top of the Swan Mountain range east of our home. With a whir of his tiny wings, the broad-tailed hummingbird called Shine arrives on the flowering landscape to begin his daily feeding ritual. He chirps repeatedly as he travels from blossom to blossom on the hanging planter. Through this vocalization, the hummingbird relays a variety of circumstances to other birds. Commonly communicating on topics from feeding to potential threats to a parent calling its offspring, the hummingbird at times also produces fast, high-pitched chirps as a way to defend its territory.

On this day, though, it is as if Shine chirps to pronounce sheer delight at the state he finds himself in. Surrounded by all that he loves, an abundance of brightly colored, nectar-filled flowers, he declares his jubilance from the depth of his little heart. In the presence of the hummingbird, I find that I cannot help but feel the connection as his apparent spark of joy now resonates within me.

*G*ratitude has an energy all its own. It is the feeling of thankfulness that is only fully realized through expression. As our minds cannot be in two opposing states, negative and positive, at the same time, I often refer to gratitude as the "super shift maker." Think about it for a moment. It is not possible to feel grumpy, angry, sad, cheated, mad, or unappreciated when we are grateful. Therefore, when we recognize that we are in a negative state, we need only make the conscious choice to acknowledge what we are grateful for. This act alone will shift our energy to a positive state. Gratitude broadens our focus by taking our minds off our troubles. As a side benefit, while we are in a state of appreciation, we feel good. It is as if gratitude lightens the soul.

I have practiced gratitude in a number of ways in my own life. From the time I get up in the morning, I begin expressing appreciation through silent devotion for all that is around me—my cozy bed, warm and wonderful home, the man lying next to me who shares my days, and all the people in my life who enrich my journey. I send thoughts of love and tenderness to those I know to be struggling, as well as those who are high on life and doing well. I keep "perfect moments" close to me, and I recall them regularly when I want a boost to my day. I find that the simple act of recalling those perfect moments creates a flutter in my heart, almost a feeling of falling in love; that is the best way I can describe what gratitude does for me. You might be asking, "What is a perfect moment?" Let me share one of mine with you now.

I opened the diary that is my life this morning, and began again with the words I am grateful.

As I dressed for my day, I pulled a very special locket out of my jewelry box, and as I clasped it around my neck, I began to smile. I recalled receiving the locket one Christmas from my stepson

Brandon on behalf of his children, my incredible grandchildren whom we affectionately refer to as the M&Ms. The necklace is lovely in its simplicity, a round glass locket on a beautiful silver chain. What makes it so special is that it came with seven charms to go inside, picked especially for me by the M&Ms. I recall placing the charms inside the locket as I studied each one and wondered how it came to be selected.

Four-year-old Madison chose a butterfly, a star, a sparkly-eyed owl, and the letter "M" to represent herself in my locket. Five-year-old Mason chose a letter "M" also, a heart inscribed with the words "Grandma," and a small blue shield inscribed with the word "Police" to represent his selections in my locket.

I made a Skype video call to thank the kids for the wonderful gift, and I spoke with Brandon first. I shared my delight with him, and told him how much it meant to me to wear the locket. I said that I planned to use the locket as an anchor for him and the kids. Each time I want to connect with them during the day, I can reach for it and clasp it in my hand as I allow my thoughts to drift to them. I shared with Brandon how sweet I thought the charms were, and out of curiosity, asked how it was that Mason had picked a police badge for me. Brandon laughed heartily and said, "You have no idea how hard I tried to talk him out of that one, but he insisted. I said to him, 'Mason, let's choose a different one—Grandma Sherri might not like that charm.'" According to Brandon, Mason was absolutely insistent on the police badge. After a couple of attempts to change his mind, Mason, feeling he may not get his wish, began to cry. "Well, that settled it, Sher," Brandon told me. "You became the proud owner of a police badge charm. I hope you like it."

"I *love* it!" I declared, "And I want to tell Mason so." Brandon called the kids to the computer from the bedroom where they were playing. I showed them I was wearing the beautiful locket they had given me, and I gushed over how amazing it was. The two of them beamed brightly with delighted smiles. I mentioned each of the seven charms they had selected, and when I got to the final one, I said, "Mason, I love the police badge. That was such a great idea to get it for me, and I wonder . . . what made you think to choose it?" Without hesitation, he answered, "Because police save people,

Grandma." My heart soared as Mason gave me a *perfect moment!* My voice wavering with emotion, I said, "Thank you, Mason. Even grandmas need a little saving now and then."

What perfect moments have you experienced? How might you create a way to keep those moments close to you, so that in an instant you can have total recall of your joy-filled experience?

In addition to the perfect moments practice, following are two simple gratitude practices that have been around awhile which I regularly recommend to clients:

- Gratitude Journal—Keep a daily journal in any way that feels right for you. You may jot down bullet points, or doodle a few notes to remind you of what you are grateful for throughout your day, or journal a paragraph or two that captures all of your thoughts and feelings.

- Gratitude Tree—Gather a few fallen branches or bare stems from a shrub and put them in a vase. Create paper leaves that you can write on and tie to the branches to "leave" some gratitude on your tree every day. Consider "growing" a gratitude tree in your home and one at your workplace. *Gratitude tree kits are also available for purchase from a number of sources online, if you wish to go that route.*

And one more! As a youngster I maintained a *feel-good* box which became the model for a gratitude tool called the *Treasure Chest*:

- Treasure Chest—Find a small jeweled box or create a special coffer you will enjoy seeing as you display it in a prominent place—on your desk or bureau. Each day seek to acquire riches to add to your treasure chest such as *inspirational quotes, a personal note from a loved one, or a special memento.* Any small trinket that upon reflection, brings you joy—is right for your treasure chest. Use your imagination, guided by your heart to recall your treasures each time you open the box!

There is a very inspiring transformation that takes place with most people who maintain a gratitude practice. Often when beginning such a practice, people search for *things* to be grateful for. Over time, they start to notice their gratitude for the *people, experiences,* and *circumstances* that enrich their lives. As they gain understanding of the power gratitude has to improve their lives in all areas, they begin to express gratitude for all that is in their lives, even that which, on the surface, looks to be anything but a blessing.

Through the act of acknowledging and celebrating the good around us with gratitude, we move away from the endless stream of unconscious negative thoughts running through our minds. We tend to find what we look for in life, so when we intentionally look for good, that is often what we find. If you buy into this idea of finding what we look for in life, why would you ever choose to look for anything but the good?

Aside from the deliberate act of taking up a gratitude practice, consider all of the ways you can open yourself to experiences that will bring more reasons for you to feel grateful. I recommend that you find as many ways as possible to enjoy nature in all its forms. By spending time in nature, you draw closer to your own true nature. See what comes up for you as you approach each encounter in the great outdoors with pure wonder, as if seeing something for the very first time.

> Look deep into nature, and then you will understand everything better.
> —Albert Einstein

Recall a time when you were captivated by a sight that was so remarkable that you were awestruck. You might have been witnessing something powerful like a giant ocean wave crashing onto the beach, or a thing of beauty such as a bright orange setting sun slipping quietly through a cloudy sky. Perhaps you caught sight of a natural wonder or phenomenon like Old Faithful Geyser erupting in Yellowstone Park, or you stood at the precipice overlooking the Grand Canyon. What do you recall about the feeling that emerged for you in that moment? Do you remember being amazed, delighted, ecstatic, speechless, or humbled? Perhaps you felt something else altogether. Did your heart skip a beat or beat a little faster? It may have been a spontaneous reaction and expression of joy, or possibly it was *love?* C'mon now, don't we all have a love of nature? Maybe it is a reminder that we are but small specks on this planet of ours. Even so, I believe our ability to positively impact those around us is enormous.

Whatever strong emotion we experience when struck by the beauty of nature or the love of a grandchild, connecting with it creates a *place mark* in time. With it, we can easily retrace and recall what we saw and felt in the past.

Do you notice how an awesome encounter with nature will completely clear your mind of the noise and clutter of the day? It is like a mental vacation. If you listen closely, you might even hear your soul whisper, "Ah-h-h . . ." *What a lovely thought.* We have all heard it said that nature restores and rejuvenates, which may explain why so many of us are drawn to travel and explore the world's many natural wonders each year. Short of that, we can be found walking, biking, hiking, swimming, camping, skiing, or doing whatever we can to fully immerse ourselves in the outdoors. So what happens to us while in nature? I like to think we are so surprised and delighted by our surroundings that we are snapped *wide awake* into the present moment. Gone are all of the worries about things past or concerns about the future. We are left with only the here and now of the present moment—and yes, it feels good.

> Keep close to Nature's heart . . . and break clear away, once in a while, and climb a mountain or spend a week in the woods. Wash your spirit clean.
> —John Muir

Living in Montana, I find I am often awestruck; unexpected encounters with wildlife and glimpses of spectacular vistas can happen at any moment. I will share one experience with you now to help stir your thoughts about some of the exceptional moments you have experienced.

It was around 4 a.m. on a cold, clear November morning when Tucker our ten-week-old Lab puppy, began to whine. He clearly needed to go outside, and knowing the importance of quickly getting him outdoors to stay on track with his housebreaking, I jumped out of bed. My winter coat and boots were still by the front door where I had left them a few hours earlier after what I thought would be our last outing of the night. I slipped them on once again as I picked up little Tucker while heading out the door. The minute I stepped outside, I felt the bitter November cold envelop me, and I tugged my coat collar up around my face and ears. Longing to be back in the cozy comfort of my warm bed, I placed Tucker down in the snow-covered meadow, hoping he would hurry up and do his job. Instead, he began to playfully wander around as if it were the middle of the afternoon. *Oh man,* I thought, *was this a trick to get me outside at this hour?* Frustrated, I contemplated scooping him back up to carry him inside when just then, my spunky little pup ran straight between my legs and stopped a few feet behind me. He began rounding his back and squatting down low. Aha! This was an actual "business trip" after all. As I turned to face his direction, something bright caught the corner of my eye. Glancing north toward the horizon, I was momentarily stunned at a sight I had never witnessed before. I caught my breath as the most brilliant green light shimmered and undulated, like sparkling emeralds in the night sky. Aurora borealis—*the northern lights!* The cold receded as I was transfixed by the beauty before me. *How spectacular!* My eyes welled with tears as I contemplated the good fortune that had brought me to this unforgettable place in time. Tucker came to me a moment later, signifying that he was done with his duty and ready to go back inside. I praised and petted him, taking my time to remain outside just a few minutes more, enjoying the mesmerizing light show. And now I felt *grateful* to my four-legged friend for waking me in the wee hours of a cold November morn.

How might such experiences with nature actually be good for us? Aside from the obvious benefits of feeling blissful and contented in the midst of the experience, we draw benefit from shifting our energy to its highest state. Moments before I saw those northern lights, my energy was low. I was feeling tired, frustrated, cold, and somewhat silly, believing I had just been tricked by my puppy to take him out in the middle of the night to play. After seeing the lights, I felt exhilarated—enchanted even. My state of mind had shifted, and with it my attitude was transformed.

By experiencing the shift that takes place in us at such times, we can understand that this benefit is a tool we can use any time we wish to create a shift in our state of mind. We can intentionally place ourselves in a position to regularly experience the wonders of nature, and anything else that brings us joy. We can also surround ourselves with reminders of our most joyful times past through the use of pictures and memorabilia.

Think of the ways your current environment supports and reminds you of your joyful spirit. Perhaps you feel inspired to feather your nest a little more now, to draw in meaningful objects that will remind you of your joy on a regular basis. *Fantastic idea!*

When you engage in your own passion and joyous nature to become a better you, by extension you better the world around you. This is, in essence, how we *become* the change we wish to see in the world. *To live in a joyous world, we must* be *joyous.*

What better gift can you give to yourself and those around you than to embody a life filled with gratitude and joy?

Worksheet Fifteen:
Gratitude Naturally

What Treasures are you are most grateful for today?

_____
_____
_____
_____
_____

How do you share your gratitude with others in your life?

_____
_____
_____
_____
_____

List the five people closest to you, and the qualities they possess that you are most grateful for.

_____
_____
_____
_____
_____

List the three most difficult relationships you have, and what it is
about those relationships that you can find to be grateful for.

_____

_____

_____

_____

_____

Describe a favorite memory or a perfect moment.

_____

_____

_____

_____

What experiences in your life are you most grateful for?

_____

_____

_____

_____

What do you do currently to put yourself in a position to regularly
experience and express your joyous nature?

_____

_____

_____

_____

Life Lesson Sixteen

Knowing When to Trust

One summer day Larry was working on a project in our garage. After a while, I went out to check on him. I sat near him on a stool so we could visit for a few minutes as he worked. Suddenly, out of the corner of my eye, I caught a glimpse of something. Oh! There it was, flying past again. Oh no! One of our hummingbird friends was inside the garage with us! Earlier that morning, Larry had propped the garage door open while he moved things around to create space to work, and apparently during that time, one of the hummers flew in and became trapped inside. We scrambled into action, trying to free the little one. It was clear he had exhausted himself flying around inside the dormer of the garage, attempting to get out through a sealed window. We were unsure of what to do next because opening the garage door only caused him to retreat to the dormer again.

What happened next still makes my heart skip a beat when I recall it. Larry grabbed a ladder, and I watched as he climbed cautiously to the top. At first the hummer appeared frightened at his approach, flying faster around and around the small space. Then, once Larry was within a few feet of the hummer, he reached his right arm up as high as he could and opened the palm of his hand. Within seconds, the bird landed softly on his outstretched palm. There he rested, calmly, trusting with his life that Larry would show him the way out. With his hand full of feathered treasure held high over his head, Larry slowly climbed down the ladder while I carefully opened the side door. We both sighed with relief a moment later as the little bird rose from the palm of Larry's hand and flew off to his home in the pines.

When we approach life with the belief that everyone around us is doing the best they can, right where they are on their own personal journey, our mind-set reflects our inner strength. From this position of strength, we see the good in others and we continually look for possibilities to adapt and grow, regardless of the circumstances we find ourselves in.

When we approach life in the opposite way, not believing others are doing the best they can, our mind-set becomes a reflection of our own vulnerability: we are constantly watching, waiting, and expecting *the other shoe to drop*. We anticipate others will come up short and let us down in some way.

If we aspire to have great relationships, we will endeavor to find ways to open up and have the courage to trust others. This becomes easier when we acknowledge the reality that from time to time we are all going to slip up, slide back, or tumble and fall. We know this is true in our lives, and when we extend that understanding to others, we allow for a little *wiggle room*. With wiggle room we can acknowledge our imperfections without judgment and set realistic expectations for ourselves and those around us.

The question becomes *How do we know whom to trust, and when we should trust them?*

There are a couple of approaches most of us have when it comes to placing trust in others:

We trust people unless and until they give us a reason not to. To some, this may seem to be a lesson in naivety, while others believe as Ralph Waldo Emerson shared, *"Trust men and they will be true to you; treat them greatly, and they will show themselves great."* When we choose to look for the best in others, fully expecting to find it, we often do.

Or

We trust people just a little, primarily regarding things that cannot harm us if that trust is breached. We build trust as the other person shows they will honor that trust. This is a common approach for many, especially in the work environment. A new employee is fully entrusted with the responsibility of their job once they have gone through training and learned the necessary skills.

Or

We trust no one and have difficulty forging close connections because trust building is an integral part of the bonding that is required to build healthy relationships.

Maybe you are shaking your head now and saying, "You have no idea what I have been through—most people just cannot be trusted!" or "Actually, the full weight of my job came down on me from the first day, so apparently I am trustworthy!" Okay, I acknowledge both scenarios, whether someone you thought you knew broke your trust or you began a job with the proverbial trial by fire! I am familiar with these issues and commend you for hanging tough through those life challenges. They may represent character building at its best!

Based upon your own life experience and what you have gleaned from relationships in the past, you will formulate trust and build relationships from what you have already learned. If you see that you are among a circle of people with integrity, strong moral character, and ethics, you will feel confident placing your trust in others.

If, on the other hand, you have experienced inconsistent behavior or broken trust by those in your circle, you are apt to withhold trust from new acquaintances and others until they have proven themselves worthy—and perhaps not even then. If you have had a tough go of things in life, suffered tremendous hardships due to untrustworthiness at the hands of others, trust may be most challenging for you.

By examining these scenarios, we can understand that trust goes hand in hand with responsibility. When we place trust in others, or they choose to trust us, we are charged with the responsibility to make that trust a reality. How we choose to express our understanding of this trust, by either upholding or disregarding that responsibility, will define our character and reputation.

What are the basic characteristics we look for in order to establish trust? We look for qualities such as these:

Reliability
Dependability
Sincerity
Credibility
Believability
Authenticity
Compassion
Honesty
Levelheadedness
Steadfastness
Unwavering, rock-solid character

Once we decide a person is worthy of our trust, we let our guard down, either gradually or all at once. Everything that an individual does from then on to demonstrate and support those "trusting qualities" serves to strengthen and build the trust in the relationship. How important is that process to our relationships? Without trust building, a relationship will not grow, but with trust building it becomes stronger and more resilient as a result.

With this added strength and resilience, we can even manage through some minor breakdowns in trust. If someone has demonstrated their reliability in the past and then one day, out of the blue, is a "no show" for an important event, we do not jump to the conclusion that they should no longer be trusted. Instead we believe this to be out of character and imagine there were extenuating circumstances that kept them from keeping their commitment. If over the course of time, however, the reliability issue continues, it will indeed begin to erode the trust in the relationship.

It takes far less effort to maintain the trust of those around us through our steadfast support of trustworthy behavior than to rebuild trust that has broken down as a result of inconsistent or unreliable behavior. This is why we never want to take another person's trust in us lightly. Trust at the most basic level is nothing other than someone having *faith* in us, and the *belief* that we will do the right thing. Is that not a compliment of the highest order?

Recently I had the pleasure of coaching two charismatic, go-getter female business partners. The two had come to me when they reached a bottleneck to growing their startup business. They were feeling very torn about what to do next, as their original business model had to change in order to meet the needs of their ideal target clients. These were their bread-and-butter clients, paying all of the bills. Although this shift promised to yield great results in the long term, the two women felt that by moving their focus away from the concepts that had brought them together in the beginning, they would be leaving their original clients in the lurch—they were adamant they did not wish to do this. Those original clients, it turns out, were receiving a ton of value for very little monetary investment on their part. The partners had created tremendous content for them, along with a number of ways to connect to others who shared their business interests.

As I coached the partners through the vision they held for their business, now and in the future, it became clear that something had to give. The amount of time and effort required to grow their company and continue with their community outreach was considerably more than they could manage. "Well, not really," said one of the partners. "As long as we continue to work until midnight seven days a week, and give up seeing our families ever again, I think we can continue on just like we are right now." A little nervous laughter followed—or maybe it was not nervousness I was detecting, but rather giddiness brought on by months of sleep deprivation. I laughed, too, coming from an all-too-understanding place in my own heart. What I know for certain about most women is that there is just no limit to what we won't do to help others, including but not limited to putting our own best interests on the back burner so we can help out.

Through coaching, the partners came to the agreement that it was time to bring in reinforcements. Here is where the issue of *knowing when to trust* emerged. The business was a labor of love for these women, an expression of the passion the two shared, and the idea of bringing in others to assist them was *scary*. So what happened next? The "what ifs" started showing up, right on schedule.

What if they don't do business the same way we do? What if they don't have the same ideas, passion, and desire to help others?

I asked the partners to share with me any examples they had of successfully joining forces with others in their existing business. It turned out they were already collaborating with others in a number of ways through social media. As they shared those successes with me, it was as if a light popped on! "Aha!" they said. "We are already effectively doing this, so it should be easy to extend our collaboration in other ways."

From there, it was as if the energy in the room catapulted to an all-time high. They began rattling off all of the ways they could use collaborative assistance to continue to grow their business, continue to provide the outreach to their original customers, *and* focus on the segment of their business that would allow them to prosper most. Whew! Now that was a win/win if ever I heard one! This time the giddiness I was detecting from the partners was something different: a renewed excitement about the possibilities for them to move forward in a way that demonstrated they were "walking their talk" while also benefiting as others benefited.

> Trust is letting go of the needing to know all the details before you open your heart.
> —Author Unknown

One week after my coaching session with the two business partners, I received a lovely note from them describing how the horizon had changed dramatically, and that they could see endless possibilities before them. How delightful for them to make that shift! By *knowing when to trust others*, they had accessed a door that previously appeared to be closed to them.

In summary, when people put their heads and hearts together, extending trust for the purpose of creating great results, wonderful things happen! Relationships grow stronger, and people operate from their peak potential. Imagine a world where everyone is performing to the best of their ability, at their peak every day. Wow! What a world that will be.

Together let's create that reality!

Worksheet Sixteen:
Knowing When to Trust

What is your philosophy when it comes to placing trust in others?

_____

_____

_____

_____

_____

Describe how effective you are at building trust in relationships.

_____

_____

_____

_____

_____

What behaviors do you regularly engage in to build trust?

_____

_____

_____

_____

_____

What habits, if any, might you engage in that break trust down?

_____

_____

_____

_____

_____

How might you step out of your comfort zone to allow someone
else to help you now? Consider areas outside of your own expertise, or those areas you don't enjoy—but others might.

_____

_____

_____

_____

_____

What would it take for you to allow for someone to help you?
(For example, I would have to give up my need to control the
outcome, or accept that someone else will do it differently, and
that is okay.)

_____

_____

_____

_____

_____

Life Lesson Seventeen

Fight Fairly

One of the most admirable of all of the hummingbird's traits is the way individuals fight with each other so that no one really gets hurt. There is a lot of vocalization—birds speaking their minds, as it were—and then, if their warning calls do not produce the desired outcome, a chase ensues.

This morning I watched a fight between two hummers that began with a chase near the roof of the house: seeming locked together in twisting flight, they spiraled downward, touching down on the deck before flying upward again. This spiral chase was immediately followed with one hummer executing a U-shaped dive, plummeting thirty or forty feet during this display while making loud buzzing and whistling sounds. I am unsure of what he was communicating to the other bird, but in hummingbird speak, that was a heated one!

From a human standpoint, how might we fight fairly within our relationships in a way that fully communicates our message without hurting one another in the process? It is possible, but only when we keep our own personalities and egos in check, and that is easier said than done. How does our ego show up in our lives? The ego is always hungry, and it wants to be fed a steady diet of recognition, attention, and validation. Simply put, it desires proof that it is alive and well—and in charge! We have to know that we are right because the ego demands it, and we may go to extraordinary lengths to get others to confirm it.

The need to be right is so ingrained in the sense of self that it transcends everything else; we will take it to the mat with anyone who dares get in our way. When we hold the mistaken belief that being right will make us happy, we can easily wreak havoc in our lives, because this means we must do whatever it takes to be right—including doing serious damage to our relationships or even ending them to prove a point. This belief and the actions that result from it actually prevent people from being happy. Think about it. It can be frustrating and exasperating to be around a person who has to be right in every conversation or transaction.

Through its need to be right, the ego requires that we sit in judgment, of ourselves and others. This adversely impacts our energy because when we judge, we are coming from a place of lack. We believe that we are being objective and that the way we see things is right, when in reality our perception of the world around us is ours alone. Another person's perception may be completely different and also be right for them.

When we judge, we affix convenient labels like *good* and *bad* to everything and everyone. We may label someone with a differing opinion bad when, after exhausting much effort, we cannot seem to get them to see how right we are. Our ego finds their refusal to acquiesce to our point of view maddening.

Where does this lack of understanding of and tolerance for a person with different views lead us? Our focus narrows, our negativity spreads, and we lose our ability to be a positive force in the life we all share. How boring life would be if we all had the same ideas, held the same opinions, and made the same choices. We would all drive the same car, live in the same house, and marry the same person. Wait . . . what? Okay, you get my point.

If we measure our own success against what we see others doing, we move into a competitive mind-set that has us judging ourselves as either a winner or a loser based on how we believe we stack up against them. If someone else does something we perceive as better than what we think we can do, we feel "less than." We feel small. The ego reaffirms our internal negative self-talk by saying, "That person is better than me, and therefore I am not good enough."

Instead of judging yourself and others, choose to measure your success by the amount of passion you have for what you are doing, and rest assured that no one else is competing in the contest to become a better you!

It takes practice and awareness to see this egocentric behavior at work and try a different approach. The opposite of judging things as good or bad is to abstain from judging them at all. Let's accept that things are what they are and realize that our need to be in control is our ego asserting itself. There is no need to control anything, and we do not need to obey the ego. Free of expectations of how we think things *should* be and what others *should* be doing, we will experience fewer disappointments and greater peace.

Sometimes even things that appear to be wrong are, in their own way, right. The mastery comes when we go beyond being thankful for what is good when we are right, and learn to see what is good about what initially appears to be wrong. Have you learned something new? Have you grown in understanding, developed tolerance, or become more patient?

Each day, as we become a little more aware of our judgment of self and others, we can consciously choose not to judge at all. Seeing ourselves and others for the best of who we truly are, without any labels, frees us to experience life to the fullest extent possible.

As we become more adept at letting go of the ego, we increasingly experience a life in which we are less afraid. *Our minds, no longer clouded with thoughts of judgments, make way for feelings of acceptance of self and others.* We will notice our ego grow in a different way, manifesting as a strong sense of self. A strong sense of self is really our "letting go" of ego, which culminates in self-mastery and a focus on bettering our own lives. This will be evident to others as we exhibit the positive, caring, and uplifting actions of someone who has become very comfortable with the process of their life unfolding.

How comfortable are you with the way your life is unfolding? Do you recognize the times when you feel inferior, or sensitive to the judgment of others? Do you notice that when you feel confident, sassy, and full of spunk, very little of what others do or say bothers you? Even when they display negative or judgmental behavior, you find that you are completely and utterly unimpressed by it. During those times of strength, notice that you are well aware of others actions, and also aware that you are choosing to be unaffected by them. You are overflowing with positive energy, and it shows. What insight does this provide for you?

On the opposite side of the coin, when you are already feeling vulnerable, sensitive, tired, or under the weather, it takes very little to trigger feelings of insecurity or uneasiness within you. It is during those times that others may push your buttons or get on your nerves, and you are apt to react poorly to a challenge. You may lash out or say something in the heat of the moment that you later regret. During those times, you do not fight fairly, and you may hurt others as a result.

Whatever is begun in anger ends in shame.
—Benjamin Franklin

Oh, boy, you can have a long river of forgiveness to swim when you burn a bridge or hurt another heart in the heat of the moment. Hence the question becomes "What am I willing to do differently to realize a better end result?"

As a start, you can begin to understand that what someone says and does is all about them, even when it is directed at you. This concept can be difficult to grasp, especially when someone is attacking you personally. It has been said that *hurting people hurt other people and are easily hurt by them.* Someone who is hurting often communicates that pain through anger: red-faced, pointing, and accusing.

In such a moment, you can make the choice to access your ability to hover above the situation and regain the proper perspective. With the awareness that when you feel strong, you have the power to turn away from actions you wish to reject, you can see that you have this ability at all times. It is simply a choice you make. Granted, it may take a little additional effort when you are feeling vulnerable, but the ability to make a great choice is always there within you.

> Holding on to anger is like grasping a hot coal with the intent of throwing it at someone else; you are the one who gets burned.
> —Buddha

With your hovering perspective, you can choose not to take on someone else's anger, but rather to observe and reflect on all that is unfolding: *Wow, what can I learn from them and about myself in this moment? How much of the upset is about what they are actually saying, and what more might be going on right now?*

Then you can do some self-reflection, asking, *What is going on with me that I am feeling so sensitive and so vulnerable?* Think about how you can be kinder to yourself and offer yourself more grace. Allow that, *yes,* you are going to be tired from time to time, vulnerable, feeling under the weather and not up to par—and that is okay.

See your life as an unfolding, and understand that constant striving for perfection is senseless. Strive instead for excellence in all that you do, excellence that you will attain when your heart and mind are in the right place.

When you let go of judging yourself and others, you will enjoy more positive energy and peace of mind. You may notice that you breathe more easily, experience less stress, and feel the weight of your worries tumbling from your shoulders. That is what acceptance feels like—a knowing that each of us is simply amazing just the way we are, imperfections and all.

Worksheet Seventeen:
Fight Fairly

What relationships challenge you the most?

_____
_____
_____
_____
_____

What are the dynamics at play within those relationships?

_____
_____
_____
_____
_____

How do you see ego showing up in your own life?

_____
_____
_____
_____
_____

How do you show up during an argument or challenge at home?
At work?

_____

_____

_____

_____

_____

What default behaviors do you exhibit when involved in a conflict?

_____

_____

_____

_____

_____

What are you willing to do differently going forward to realize a
better end result?

_____

_____

_____

_____

_____

Life Lesson Eighteen

File Your Flight Plan

The hummingbird knows his way, and he flies the same migration route year after year from south to north and back again. He follows his annual plan according to his instincts and allows them to guide him safely along to his destination.

A few years ago my grandfather was visiting our home from south central Montana. He got a kick out of watching the hummingbirds, and we shared some light-hearted conversation about their personalities and behavior as we sat together on the deck one summer morning. I recall curiously musing, to no one in particular, "I wonder where they migrate to and from each year. I have heard stories of hummers traveling hundreds and hundreds of miles to cross the Mojave Desert and the open sea to get to their seasonal homes. How can they possibly fly so far?"

Without hesitation, my grandfather said, "The hummers migrate on the backs of geese." His answer seemed pretty farfetched to me, and I raised my eyebrows straight up as if to question his statement as I looked him in the eye. In response he declared, "It's true!" The image this idea created for me was one I rather enjoyed, like an illustration in a children's bedtime story. I envisioned the hummingbirds nestled inside the soft, downy feathers of their hosts, the geese, as they were transported safely across the country. My grandfather was so sincere in his declaration, in that moment a part of me regis-

tered the hope that he would never learn the truth about the hummers' solitary migration. I said nothing to challenge his logic or dispel the myth as we both looked on and smiled.

here are you migrating next? What a funny question to ask a person! You are probably not migrating unless you are part of a nomadic tribe, and likely you would not be reading this book if you were. Let's put travel plans aside for a moment, then, and talk about where you are headed in the next year or so with respect to your goals.

The late songwriter and composer Jonathan Larson wrote the hit song "Seasons of Love" for the Broadway musical *Rent*. His lyrics seem to beg us to consider how to best quantify the value of a human life in a year. How would you say you quantify your last *five hundred twenty-five thousand six hundred minutes?* Was this year all you had hoped it would be? In terms of the vision you had as the year began and how it stacked up at the end against what you had intended for yourself, would you say it was a success?

How do you see yourself when it comes to managing goal setting and realization? Some people are pretty adept at setting goals for their work. It may be that this is a requirement in your career, and therefore something you regularly participate in. *Great!* Know that what works on the job works on the home front as well. If you are not in the habit of creating goals, there is no time like the present to start!

Why set goals? Without goals and a system for measuring our success, we tend to whittle away our days in trivial ways. We become loyal to our daily habits and routines regardless of whether they are the best use of our time, and we simply continue to do what we have always done, because we have always done it.

Far away there in the sunshine are my highest aspirations. I may not reach them, but I can look up and see their beauty, believe in them, and try to follow where they lead.
—Louisa May Alcott

Having clearly defined goals and a sense of your broader purpose will provide a focal point and the energetic commitment required to accomplish what you want in your lifetime. Upon reaching your goals, you will realize pride for a job well done and increase your confidence in your ability to achieve even more in the future. I love this quote from Henry David Thoreau: "What you get by achieving your goals is not as important as what you become by achieving your goals." To me, that is the essence of the real reason for goals; they require us to continue to stretch our abilities, to further advance, learn and grow.

Having goals lights your inner fire. Instead of just wishfully thinking about what you want, setting goals and accountabilities for those goals compels you to get going. The more specific your goals are, the better chance you have of reaching them. Specificity adds clarity to your desires, and accountability sheds light on whether you are living up to what you committed yourself to doing when you first set your goal. With your goals in mind, you develop ways to become accountable for them. This accountability is what you use as a measure of your success when you opt to stay the course and forgo any short term gratification you might gain by ditching your goals on any given day. It is what you answer to when you spend an afternoon working industriously on your plans and projects rather than socializing with friends or colleagues. *Goals will help you reach your peak potential by providing targets to aim for.* Without goals, you act from your normal, accepted routine, day in and day out. If you are always working within your comfort zone, you avoid actions beyond the ordinary. Bear in mind that the comfort of routine runs contrary to your personal growth, and staying within your comfort zone does not enable you to become your personal best. Rather, it stymies your growth and prevents you from maximizing the vast capability inside of you. It is only by reaching beyond your normal competencies that you develop personal accomplishments and achievements you were not previously aware you could reach, or pursue opportunities you otherwise would have missed.

Think about how setting goals can help you elevate your game in all areas of your life. Career goals ensure you are striving to better your skills and abilities rather than accepting something less. A friend once said to me, *"If you have to work eight hours a day, you may as well make the most money that you can while you are there."* Well, is that not the truth? When you set fitness goals and track them over a period of several months, you can accurately gauge your effectiveness at achieving your desired fitness level. The more goal- and action-oriented you are, the more success you will have.

Goal setting need not be complicated. The process is as easy as 1, 2, 3.

1. Decide what you want and then write it down. Writing your goals is an important part in the process of realization, as it brings the goal out of the realm of the imagination and into the realm of reality. Get clear on your goals so that you can measure your success.

    It is not a clear goal to say you want to save money for a down payment on a new car. Figure out the amount you will need and go from there.

    A clear goal is *I will save $12,000 toward the down payment on my new car.*

2. Next, create action steps that will help you move toward your goals. If they are large, you may need to take a number of steps to get there, and therefore you may have smaller goals or milestones you wish to achieve along the way. To apply that to the down payment example: *I will save $150 from my paycheck twice a month for twenty-four months, and put an additional $200 per month in my savings account from my allocated discretionary spending, to reach my $12,000 goal.*

3. Set a deadline for your goals. *I will begin saving this month, and achieve my goal in twenty-four months, keeping a monthly savings log to track my progress.*

As you consider the types of goals you wish to set, remember to think in terms of both short- and long-term goals. Short-term goals have time frames of a day, a week, or a few months. Long-term goals are those broader life goals that may take a year, or two, or five, or ten to realize.

Short-term goals will help you to create the regular habit of goal setting and accountability. Right away, you will begin to measure your success as you move the needle in the areas you most desire to improve. Watching that needle move will provide you with motivation as you propel forward. With each short-term goal reached, you can measure your gains toward the broader life goals you plan to achieve.

If you regularly set short- and long-term goals, perhaps you have already given some thought to where you will be five years from now. You may have goals and action plans that will lead you year by year toward a five-year vision you have for yourself.

Look back now, five years in time. It may seem like an eternity, but in truth it was just a blink of an eye. What transpired in those previous five years to bring you to this moment in time? Were you following a well-laid plan during that five-year period, while perhaps making a few adjustments to that plan as changes came your way? If so, where you are at this moment is probably, more or less, where you envisioned yourself to be. Terrific!

When I look in my own five-year rearview mirror, it is a reminder of how quickly time flies. Five years ago, I was firmly entrenched in my corporate hospitality career and beginning to feel the call to move on after twenty-two years in the same line of work. It was not an overnight transition, leaving the only work I had ever known. Once I made the decision that it was time to move on, I went about acquiring additional skills and abilities while simultaneously researching what I would do next.

My broad goal was to find a career that would allow me to play to my passion for helping others and my strength for identifying and eliciting the best in those around me. To some degree, throughout my career I had been doing just that at every opportunity, and now I was ready to immerse myself in the pursuit of that passion full time. The more I researched and developed my goals, the more clarity I received as they took shape. In 2010, I launched my own business and followed my calling to become a certified professional coach. I could not feel any happier or be more fulfilled had I settled in to my old comfort zone and remained there for the balance of my career.

Today, I understand that what was true five years ago is true again now. I am right where I am supposed to be at this very moment in my life. Everything I did in my past prepared me and led me to this place. My current five-year vision is clearly in my sights, and it will undoubtedly be a stretch for me, but I have never been one to sit back and feel comfortable with the status quo. It just does not feel right for me. I enjoy learning, growing, and experiencing all that life has to offer. And I know that my big plans, when executed to the best of my ability, will further me along this amazing journey I affectionately call My Big Life!

Sometimes stepping outside your comfort zone feels like standing on the precipice of life itself. Take a deep breath and press on. *Your Big Life* is waiting just up ahead there in the distance.

Tell me, where will your flight plan lead you?

Worksheet Eighteen:
File Your Flight Plan

Get clear on the big vision you have of your life for the next one, three, and five years. Describe what you want for your life, complete with vivid details about where you see yourself, who will be there with you, and what you will be doing. Expand your senses. What do you feel, see, and hear? Make your vision rich and add as much Technicolor as you can to bring it to life.

_____

_____

_____

_____

_____

As you review your goals, what kinds of actions can you take to begin to move you in the direction of achieving those goals? The specific actions will become easier to gauge when you chunk them down from a year to monthly, weekly, and daily in size. Think of it one step at a time.

_____

_____

_____

_____

_____

Once you have your action steps, remember to orient them in time, using deadlines so you can measure your progress.

_____

_____

_____

_____

Life Lesson Nineteen

Concern Yourself with
What You Can Control

*Early in the morning, the sun is warm while the valley
air remains chilly. Although it is midsummer here in the
Flathead, it is as if spring never quite relinquished her grip.
I busy myself cleaning and refilling hummingbird feeders on
a daily basis, knowing the hummers' high-energy lifestyle
means they are on a constant quest for sources of food. They
must feed, on average, from five to eight times per hour, and
they consume about half of their body weight in sugar daily.
Much as feeders provide a ready source of nourishment for
the tiny birds, their primary diet consists of flower nectar and
small insects that provide the nutrients they require. I can
only imagine how hungry the hummingbirds must be after
a long migration from their winter homes in the south to
their summer homes here in the north. Quickly I gather the
feeders to refill the nectar, and as the birds arrive, they hover
only briefly where the feeder usually hangs before moving on.
They never linger, fret, or expend their energy needlessly over
those things that are beyond their control.*

*Y*our own ability or inability to adapt readily and willingly to changes around you will largely determine the degree of success you experience in your life. Consider now in what areas you invest your time and energy, and whether these are places where you have influence and control.

In the workplace, changes occur in every area from personnel policies and procedures to benefits and pay to company structure, organization, and ownership. Changes may come together gradually, or as happens with an acquisition or merger, they may happen rapidly, concurrent with the formation of the new entity.

If you find that you are easily drawn into dramas that unfold among colleagues or staff members, or into the situations people around you find themselves in, it is time to take a step back and ask yourself what it is about those situations that draws your attention. An even better question might be to ask, *How can I support those around me without being drawn into their story?*

Furthermore, *How might I be a positive contributor without becoming a co-conspirator?*

Changes on the home front can often be unplanned and unexpected as well, through weddings, births, and those we love passing away. We may relocate, experience changes among those close to us that affect us financially or emotionally, such as separation or divorce, go through a job loss, or endure another form of upheaval.

Change often invokes fear, especially when it is something you did not want or invite, as with a company merger or other organizational change. Unless you can find a way to work through it, this fear can make it difficult to move forward and maintain a productive and positive outlook. And allowing yourself to become entrenched in fighting against change it can cost you a tremendous amount of wasted energy.

When you are faced with change, you commonly have three choices:

Deny It

This approach rarely improves anything. Although you may choose to ignore the change, you can seldom do so for long. When you are not directly involved in shaping and influencing how change unfolds, the new circumstances that result may be even less desirable for you. At times change can be postponed, but rarely can it be denied.

Accept It

When you accept change, you are open to the events that unfold. With this receptive mind-set, you will be better able to adapt to a thought process that accommodates new possibilities. With acceptance you are better prepared for change to take place.

Find a Way to Advance Through It

This is a highly engaged approach. When you look for ways to not only accept change but also make the best of it, you will be ideally positioned to make it work for you. Quickly adapting to change helps you channel your energy into more positive outcomes. With this method you open to all the possibilities that may accompany change and will be ready for new opportunities that come to light.

Viewing change as a process and understanding that you will evolve with it helps put it into proper perspective. Rarely will you be able to flip a switch and—voilà—you and the change magically merge together and ride off into the sunset. *Au contraire.* As with most things in life, only through planning and preparation can you steady yourself to successfully navigate change.

> One change always leaves the way open for the establishment of others.
> —Niccolò Machiavelli

Perhaps you never considered how best to harmonize with change, although find you are now open to new ways of thinking.

Outstanding! The following tips will help you prepare for change.

Be alert to the signs that change may be coming. Often it is an inkling, clue, or red flag that appears to indicate something new is on the horizon. You may sense a key relationship is shifting, notice a persistent health problem with a loved one, or overhear a conversation at work. Consider the proactive steps you might take to best meet those developments if they materialize.

Drawing on the hovering lesson explained earlier in the book, act as both the observer and participant in this change. Recognize that you are embarking on a transition that is now a part of your life and the lives of those around you. This might seem simple enough, but the act of observing the situation takes you out of the thought-clouded, worrying, oh-no-I-can't-believe-this-is-happening, emotion-saturated experience.

Examine your mind-set about this change. Is it something you look forward to, something you are opposing, or feeling neutral about? If you feel resistance, buck the temptation to spend time ruminating over questions like *Why me?* and instead ask *What opportunity might be presenting itself here?* This small shift in your perspective will create the momentum required to adopt a positive mind-set during the transition.

Next, determine what concerns you have about the impending change. It might take a little digging to go beyond the obvious and get to the heart of the matter. Understand although you may not be in control of the full unfolding of events, this does not mean that you are powerless to positively impact them. Once you have a clear picture of the fears you are facing, you can dispel any that are unfounded, and set about the work of finding solutions to the bona fide ones.

Adopt the viewpoint that change is a process—allowing time for it all to unfold while you adapt to new circumstances. This viewpoint will help ease your mind while providing relief from self-imposed pressure to conform as you align yourself to the transition.

Determine that you will find a positive possibility somewhere within the change, understanding that it might not immediately present itself. If it helps to remind yourself, look back to a time in your past when you went through something that felt similar to what you are experiencing now—which turned out surprisingly well. Recall what it was about *you* that made that past change successful. Whatever strengths you drew from within yourself back then are available to you at present—call them forth again.

Practice good self-care as you are going through change. To do this, ensure you are making healthy food choices, getting plenty of rest, and vigorously exercising as recommended by your health care provider. Be mindful to maintain empowering thoughts in order to best prepare for change. Good physical well-being, a clear mind, and calm nerves will benefit you in countless ways as you make the transition.

Consider how you might create incentives for yourself to adapt to the change in order to create forward progress as it unfolds. What might you like to work toward during this time of transition? Are you learning something new, or challenging yourself to grow in some way? How might you draw benefit or reward from this change? Write it out, along with any milestones you intend to use to monitor your success.

Finally, call for reinforcements! Why not enlist the backing of a good coach, mentor, trainer, leader, or other support person to help you manage through the change and constructively direct your energy to get the most benefit out of it.

Change is like a wrapped package that only reveals the gift inside when we are open to it.

The surest way to get ahead is to concern yourself with the areas you have control over and work on those. Accept change as a part of life, taking small ones in stride where possible and adapting as quickly and positively as you can to the big ones.

Worksheet Nineteen:
Concern Yourself with What You Can Control

What changes have you gone through during the past year?

_____

_____

_____

_____

_____

How do you handle changes that are not of your own choosing?

_____

_____

_____

_____

_____

If the change is happening at work, in what ways can you continue to contribute your best performance and support the goals of the business?

_____

_____

_____

_____

_____

How do you handle changes on the home front when faced with relocations or changes in family, income, or employment?

_____

_____

_____

_____

_____

What attributes or characteristics might you develop to help you adapt better, faster, and more readily to change?

_____

_____

_____

_____

_____

If you were to see yourself as a change agent, rather than powerless to bring about change, what one change would you implement at home? At work?

_____

_____

_____

_____

_____

What is currently getting in the way of your making these changes?

_____

_____

_____

_____

_____

What would be different about your life if you made these changes?

_____

_____

_____

_____

_____

Life Lesson Twenty

Fly Forward—Don't Look Back

Zoom! The hummingbird arrives in the midst of the enormous flowering catmint. I notice that his flight path appears to be a smooth circle around the flower garden to the north, through the hanging baskets on the east, south through the blooming shrubbery, and west to the planters before returning to his home in the ponderosa pine. The hummingbirds fly with efficiency, traveling far and wide alone rather than in a flock like many bird species. For all one knows, this is so they remain less visible to birds of prey and other predators. Without so much as a glance behind him, the hummer carries on.

*W*hat direction are you heading in as you approach your work and your life? Is your movement consistently forward, or do you find that you are often drawn back to areas you thought were over and done with? Do you find that you repeat patterns from the past? Do lingering regrets tug at your sleeve? There is something enigmatic and often profound going on just below the surface with every person we meet. Although most people wear a brave face, acting as if nothing is weighing on them, we all carry burdens around with us in one form or another. Learning to lighten our load—or carry it in a more beneficial way—is our work.

As a coach, I regularly hear from clients about a disappointment or a sense of a nagging conscience they carry from their past. Often they relay a feeling of unfinished business or a desire for a chance to do something over again and handle it better than they did the first time around. Through the coaching process I help them find a purpose in their past experiences to bring forward into the present so they can view those past circumstances in a new light.

The questions become "What did you learn about yourself or others through that experience?" and "How will that learning impact your decisions or actions when you are faced with a similar experience in the future?"

We know that hindsight is 20/20, but how nice it would be to have that 20/20 view of our life in the present tense. Can you imagine writing a letter to your past self? Think about the insight you would pass on from your future self. Your letter might read something like this:

Dear Former Self,

Just a note to reassure you that there is no need to get all worked up and upset about most of the issues you see yourself facing right now. Before long you will understand that these things are not nearly as complicated as you might think, and it will all become clear soon. Go ahead, lighten up a little. Smile more and worry less. You will be glad you did.

In appreciation,
The Person You Evolve Into

How cool would it be to employ this technique in your life? Would you like to give it a try? Think about it. What letter might you send to yourself now to shift your perspective or alleviate some anxiety you might be experiencing? Drawing on the insights and knowledge you now have about events in the past, what do you wish to share?

When we can stop beating ourselves up over the past and learn to look at what happened to us then in the proper perspective—as something that we learned, survived, or overcame—we can embrace our growth and transformation.

In time, we can appreciate the fact that we are always doing the best we can with what we know at any given point in our lives.

Kelly, a client of mine, was struggling in a relationship with her boyfriend. The two of them had been on-again, off-again for several years. They were both very passionate and high spirited. When they came together, sparks flew—and not always in a positive way. Kelly told me that when it was good, it was great, and when it was bad they both suffered. They split and reunited numerous times, and within a short time of returning to the relationship, Kelly would be reminded of all of the reasons she had chosen to break the connection before.

When she was with her boyfriend, she was very unhappy. The weight of the issues the two shared were constantly on her mind, distracting her from all of the positive aspirations and goals she wanted to achieve in her own life. Her boyfriend, it seems, successfully transferred his problems to her shoulders and she willingly carried his concerns along with her own. The interesting thing was that her boyfriend was unwilling, or possibly unable, to do much of anything at all to lighten Kelly's load.

When I asked her what drew her back to this relationship time and time again, she had to give it some thought. What she shared with me was her realization that she would rather be in a relationship, even one that was volatile and unstable, than be alone.

I was intrigued to hear her say that, and you would be, too, if you knew her. Kelly had a fun, vivacious personality, and was surrounded by a large circle of loved ones, family, and friends. It appeared that she was associating being "lonely" with being "alone." Additionally, she told me that she chose the "devil she knew" versus "the devil she didn't know." To me, that sounded like she had made an assumption that every potential boyfriend she was apt to meet was likely to have similar undesirable traits as the one she was currently involved with. As I share this story about Kelly, think about the ways *assumptions* cause us to limit our actions. If we think we already know how things are going to turn out, we will not change or try anything new.

All of this insight was handy to help Kelly begin to see the reality of the alliance with her boyfriend in a new light. By uncovering her motives for continuing to return to her past, she learned that she was conjuring up fears that prevented her from moving forward to a brighter future.

She began to recognize that when she felt lonely, she only needed to pick up the phone or send an invitation to someone in her wide circle of connections and she could turn her day around. Kelly also saw that by staying in an unhealthy relationship, she had no opportunity to meet anyone new. She was closed off, and wore an "air of unavailability" around her like a shield, keeping all eligible bachelors at bay.

With this shift in perspective, Kelly was able to see a way forward again. She began finding ways to build herself up so that she was not looking outside herself for someone else to fill the void. She took classes at the college, volunteered for a community service organization, joined a gym, and made plans at least two nights a week to meet friends for dinner or attend her favorite book club. Kelly's life began to take on a brand new air. She was developing confidence and self-esteem while growing her circle of contacts and experiences.

Kelly tells me now that she feels fulfilled through community service and feels great about the way she is taking care of herself while connecting with only those people who are positive influences in her life. I imagine there is a special someone out there for Kelly. Their paths will cross at some point down the road—now that she is open and receptive to a fresh, new relationship.

> The key is to keep company only with people who uplift you, whose presence calls forth your best.
> —Epictetus

When you keep looking to the past to fill a space in your life that is otherwise uncomfortable for you, it is good to recognize your pattern of backtracking, stop for a moment, and evaluate what might really be going on. Ask what it is that keeps you moving backward rather than forward. For this process to work, you have to be willing to look objectively at any behaviors or patterns that come to the surface. It is not important to determine *how* they came to be, but rather *what* you will do about them once you have identified them.

It takes a lot of courage to break from the past, to leave the known and venture into the unknown. Your brave new world is patiently waiting to be discovered, but it is up ahead of you there in the distance, not behind you. Maintain progress one day at a time, and remember—change is a process. Keep flying forward!

Worksheet Twenty:
Fly Forward—Don't Look Back

Describe the letter you would write to your Former Self about
an issue in the past that consumed you with worry and later
turned out much better than expected. It might be something
that, although painful at the time, helped you to grow in a
remarkable way.

_____

_____

_____

_____

_____

What do you notice about the cycles or patterns in your life now?

_____

_____

_____

_____

_____

What, if anything, draws you back to repeat lessons from the past?

_____

_____

_____

_____

_____

What purpose might you find in the lessons you have learned so far, in order to break those patterns and move forward in a new way?

_____

_____

_____

_____

_____

Life Lesson Twenty-One

Be Productive

The hummingbird doesn't seem to mind another hot August day. He busily goes about his chores, tending to the flowers—and then stops midflight, concentrating on a second hummingbird that entered the area. I observe him closely, and smile as I sense his growing irritation, envisioning the wild chase that is about to ensue. The hummingbird's tendency to become easily distracted is a trait that seems directly transferable to those traits we humans share. Nothing derails our productivity quicker than an unplanned interruption. Sure enough, the hummer sounds the battle cry, and he is off—making chase around the garden with no regard to his previous agenda.

*H*ow often during the day do you find yourself distracted and taken off task by unproductive activities that are not what you intended to spend time on?

One of the most common coaching themes is this very topic. In an age when most people find that there are more tasks to accomplish in a day than the hours available to do the work, your productivity is worth looking into.

When I first began working from home after twenty-seven years in the high-intensity, stress-packed travel and tourism industry, I faced some interesting challenges. Although I had much less in the way of responsibilities, I recognized that my productivity was not what it should be. At the end of a business day, I found myself carrying work over to the next day, and by the end of the week, I was not satisfied with the amount of work I had completed. Oddly enough, I also noticed I was still experiencing stress, just as I had in my former role, which involved a great deal more responsibility and a much larger work load.

Intrigued by this self-observation, I decided to track my activity. I used a small notebook in tandem with my day planner, and each time I got sidetracked from the list of tasks I had decided to complete that day, I wrote down in the notebook what had distracted me and how much time I had spent on the distraction.

After just a half day, I found the culprit that was eating away at my productivity: *it was me!* If I needed to research something online, I allowed myself to go off course and follow whatever shiny objects caught my attention. There were a lot of interesting things to learn, but they all led to the same place—*straight down the rabbit hole ending in a giant waste of time.* My email was another huge distraction. I had set my mail server to alert me with a pop-up on my screen, and with each new alert, I toggled immediately over to email, where

I read and took action on the message regardless of its significance. Email alone was a major resource drain, and I will not even mention the time I wasted chatting on the phone during my peak productivity times. That valuable time would never be recovered.

It was curious to me that I had been so delighted to walk away from the intensity of corporate life only to re-create a variety of silly time wasters that put me behind on my tasks and duties, thus creating stress where none need exist. At the same time, I understood that I was reliving the feelings and tension that I had experienced as a successful business person in previous years, and it felt very natural to get amped up in that way. It felt so natural to me, in fact, that I was seeking to bring back that feeling when it no longer existed. Whoa! *Now that was a load of self-realization.*

> The important thing is not to stop questioning. Curiosity has its own reason for existing.
> —Albert Einstein

It is not uncommon for clients to reach out to me about productivity problems when they hit a wall. They might be facing full-on burnout, as most of them are under tremendous pressure from their mounting workload and feel overwhelmed. Once that overwhelm kicks in, it becomes difficult to focus, and without focus, the tendency is to scatter their energy.

Reflect for a moment on a time when you were overwhelmed, and recall how you were working during those times. Do you recall your energy being scattered? You might remember beginning a number of projects while having difficulty completing even the simplest of tasks. When this happens, productivity slides, and it fast becomes a slippery slope. If you find you have trouble focusing on the tasks at hand and you lack a clear vision as to where to begin, it is a clear signal that it is time to find a new approach to get past the roadblock.

First things first. Understanding that it is not possible to do everything all at once, focus on just those urgent and important tasks looming in front of you, and set them as top priorities. Next, take a bird's-eye view of the scope of all of the work to be done and jot it all down. You may create a master list of the projects to do and the tasks associated with each project. For some people, simply making a project and task list brings relief. As happens with overwhelm in any area, what we ruminate over in our minds can become larger than it actually is. Getting it out of our heads and down on paper is the first step to releasing some of the pent-up pressure. Well, shoot. That is easy enough to do, right?

After you have the list, you can set priorities, again listing the most urgent and important items at the top. Consider the time it will take for the variety of projects before you, and plan your time accordingly. If you do not already have a daily planner, online calendar, or time tracker, now would be a good time to get one. Schedule your projects on your planner and begin to take action, one item at a time.

The list is now complete. The tasks have all been prioritized, and have even found their way onto your planner. Fantastic! Are you fired up and ready to begin? How do you think you will do with this game plan tomorrow? Do you find that you are concerned about distractions, interruptions, and drains on your time and energy? Good. That means you are fully aware of those things that hijack your agenda on an average day. Now that you are aware, you can take action on those as well.

Here is the short list of common agenda hijackers and productivity drains during an average work day:

Personal phone calls

Surfing the Internet

Non work related social media

Email

Text or Instant Messaging

Disorganization

Lack of accountability

Coworkers

Unstructured conference calls

Meetings that start late or run over schedule

Meetings with no clear agenda or outcome

Meeting too frequently

When allowed to go unchecked, these productivity drains will consume your day and you will wind up with nothing much accomplished to show for it. If you find that you are busy but not as effective as you know you should be, consider tracking your time and activities for a few days to give you a clear picture of where you are spending your time. Take into account that being productive is not the same thing as being busy. Results do not lie, so be sure to examine the results you are getting to determine how effectively you are working.

Once you have a clear picture of what your productivity drains are, be sure to plug them up. Take action to minimize the distractions and time wasters so you can get back on track.

Remember, productivity drains are energy drains. You have only so much horsepower in your tank each day. You can choose to use it to drive victoriously across the finish line or use it to putt around the track, aimlessly following whatever distraction grabs your attention. *How you choose to use your horsepower is up to you. You are the driver. The key to being productive is in your hands.*

Worksheet Twenty-One:
Be Productive

List all of the drains on your time.

At work

_____
_____
_____
_____
_____

At home

_____
_____
_____
_____
_____

What valves can you close on those time drains in order to be more productive? Go for the low-hanging fruit. If something is easy to do, it will be easy to *not* do it by creating a new habit of not doing it! Let's start there.

_____

_____

_____

_____

_____

How might you maximize your productivity around those events that are beyond your control? (mandatory meetings, conference calls)

_____

_____

_____

_____

_____

During which hours of the day are you able to rev up your horsepower and do your best work?

_____

_____

_____

_____

_____

How might you schedule your most demanding projects around your most productive hours?

_____

_____

_____

_____

_____

Life Lesson Twenty-Two

Learn to Let Go

My final reflection makes me long for next summer already. It is late in the season now, and the hummingbirds appear to have migrated. There has been no activity at the feeders over the past several days. When the hornets and wasps increase their aggressive activity during this time of year, the hummingbirds let go. It is around this time that the floral highway along the upper ridge of the Rocky Mountain range begins to blossom, beckoning them to return to their southern homes for the winter. The hummingbirds do not hang on past the time that is best for them here. Recognizing there is a cycle to life and a time to move on, the hummingbird lets go.

*A*s a coach, I often listen as clients describe their desire for change while at the same time feeling unable to attain it. Holding tight to the past does not help us in the present, and as the hummingbird knows, learning to let go is the key.

When our lives are too full, it becomes hard to find the space to create the changes we want. We are simply too busy to make room for it. "How can I possibly fit this change into my day?" we ask. Great question! Rather than cramming more into the day, what might it look like to loosen our grip, and let go of a few things? If we truly desire change, we have to be willing to release the behaviors, beliefs, people, patterns, and habits that bind us to our present circumstances.

The question becomes "What am I willing to let go of in order to open up space for my desired change to occur?" The answer might be to release tangible items that have outlived their usefulness, those things that clutter your life, home, or office. If you find that the things you own have begun to own you, commanding too much responsibility and upkeep with far less enjoyment in return, it might be time to release a few of them. Consider selling or donating what goods you can to free up space in your environment—and your mind.

You may find that you need to release something intangible, like a belief, ritual, or routine. For example, a frequent coaching topic for my clients involves the way they think about, and ultimately experience *time*. If you also subscribe to the belief, *there is never enough time*, you will remain firmly rooted in a pattern of feeling pressured, under fire, and always behind schedule—because—that is what you believe! Remember, your thoughts create your feelings. When you consider, the most accomplished, and successful people in every walk of life have the same twenty-four hours per day you do, you see it's the belief *there is never enough time* that should be challenged here. The questions become, *Where am I spending my time?* And, *how does this serve my greatest aspirations?*

What if you let go of that old belief and instead adopt a new one: *There is always enough time to do what is most important to me?* How might choosing this new belief change the way you currently plan and schedule your day?

Releasing rituals and routines that no longer serve you can powerfully transform your life. What habits and routines have you formed over the years, and how might you better invest your time or resources if you were to change or eliminate them? Maybe you are not convinced that a small habit exacts much of a price. You may need to take this idea a step further to see the full value that a change in rituals and habits would bring your way.

For instance, if you are like a lot of people, you may be in the habit of stopping for coffee every morning after heading out of the house to begin your day. Let's say that on average, each visit to the coffee shop will cost you $5.00. On the surface that might not seem like a big deal, but keep in mind that you could be making your coffee for pennies a day at home—and if over the course of a year you stop for coffee twenty-five or more times per month, you will spend at least $1,500.00 on this coffee shop ritual you created. Projecting that habit out over a ten-year period, you will have spent $15,000.00 at the coffee shop. It is mind-blowing to look at it that way, right? But think about it. What did you receive in return for that coffee shop expense, aside from the short-lived buzz of caffeine? Not much!

What if you were to create a new habit of investing that same amount of money instead? The $1,500.00 you spent on coffee per year over a ten-year period, invested with a modest 6 percent return, becomes $23,643.74. *Seriously: the costs of our habits add up.* Be mindful about your habits, and invest in yourself instead!

When it comes to relationships, it might be time to learn to release the relationships or people who are holding you back.

If it is true that you take on characteristics of those people you spend the most time with, and you find that you have surrounded yourself with some who are continuously negative, gossiping, complaining, and blaming others for all that goes wrong, the chances are that you will also exhibit those qualities at some point due to frequent exposure to them. Or perhaps you will not assume those qualities, because you are bent on "fixing" those people by making them over into something they are not: namely, more positive. Although you may be well intentioned, it is not your job to change anyone else, and any attempt to do so is surely an exercise in futility. It takes a lot of energy to be in negative relationships or engulfed in negative environments all of the time. Negative energy weighs heavily on you and impacts all that you do. Like a dark cloud, another's negativity casts a shadow over you making it difficult to shine, and show up as your personal best. As I tell my clients, when a positive person is in a negative relationship, it feels a little like trying to run in a giant vat of peanut butter. Sure, you can manage to get through it, but man oh man, it is heavy, slow going! It takes tremendous effort. For that negative person in your life to change, they would have to desire to change and buy into making it happen in their own lives, and in their own time.

Regardless of the reasons you choose to stay in relationships that are not in your best interest, it is highly likely that over time, others' negativity will adversely affect you—and they will hold you back from living the highest vision you have of yourself. Life can be demanding enough without adding complexity, so consider what makes it necessary to create drama where none need exist, or to allow others to draw you into their needless dramas.

When we take full responsibility for our lives and forego any temptation to blame others, we own the power that it will take to make things over to the way we wish them to be. Walking away from the relationships and people who drain us and bring us down does not make us bad people, nor does it mean we do not care for them. It simply means we value our own well-being enough to let them go so we can move on. Also, it is possible to let go while still sending others our very best wishes. That is a great place to start. *Wish them well and on their way.*

Nothing is a waste of time if you use the experience wisely.
—Auguste Rodin

Think about how you might spend more time with positive people who are wise, ambitious, and in sync with you. Make it a goal to surround yourself with people who reflect the person you desire to be. Choose friends and companions who bring out the best in you, those you are proud to know, those you respect and care for who also respect and care for you.

Start making plans to change, and take action. If you feel some resistance, know that it is perfectly natural, as action and change are often resisted when they are needed most. Dig deep and rely on your self-discipline to stay the course and stick to the changes that will move your life forward in a powerful way. Do not procrastinate. Intention without action is just another good idea, so do not allow what you "should" be doing to rent space in your head. Decide what is most important for you to be, have, and do in your life—then go get it!

Shifting focus to what is most important will bring you clarity and lift your eyes from the path in front of you to the horizon above. You will move from being in the position of "firefighter" in the midst of the fire to that of "contractor," building and constructing your life as you desire.

Letting go of what I am, I become what I might be.
—Lao Tzu

Coming from this perspective, what might you choose to do differently in your day, your week, your month, or your year? Beginning with the most important priorities first, what will you choose to focus on?

First, you must create the space to allow change to happen. What might this space look like for you, and, more importantly, what are you willing to let go of in order to create it?

Look around—what lessons are being presented to you now? Are they coming through people who are close to you, or from somewhere in nature—like the hummingbird's ease with letting go?

As you continue along the path of self-discovery I hope from time to time you will appreciate just how far you've come. With ever increasing awareness you will be acting more and more from a place of choice, mindful of your surroundings, and conscious of the fact that most of what makes up your life story is your reaction to your life events. Acknowledge that you are beginning to perceive life differently—knowing that everything around you can be viewed as an opportunity for your growth, for more understanding, and a chance to choose the response representing the highest vision you hold of yourself.

Nature is always providing examples of how you can live your best life. You need only become still enough to notice. How do you become still? Shift your focus to your breathing as you tune in to the graceful cadence of your heart. *There!* Do you sense it beating in tandem with the rhythm of nature? *Ah, yes—there you are—rising up to hover like the hummingbird.*

Worksheet Twenty-Two:
Learn to Let Go

Describe three changes you would like to implement in your life
this year.

_____
_____
_____
_____
_____

What material possessions are you currently holding on to that
no longer serve you?

_____
_____
_____
_____
_____

What thoughts and beliefs are you aware of that may be holding
you back from living the highest vision you hold for yourself?

_____

_____

_____

_____

_____

What old habits would you like to release and replace with new
habits that are more empowering?

_____

_____

_____

_____

_____

What are you willing to let go in order to allow the time and space
for these changes to happen? (Such as out dated beliefs, old
routines, TV time, hours on social media, or Internet surfing.)

_____

_____

_____

_____

_____

The Light

By Sherri Lynea Gerek

Wherever THE LIGHT shines THE DARKNESS will fade.

Oh, but THE DARKNESS will protest loudly, and angrily at THE LIGHT

As THE LIGHT goes on shining.

THE DARKNESS will double up its fists as THE LIGHT approaches, *You will not change me.*

And still THE LIGHT continues to shine.

THE DARKNESS will scream and rage at THE LIGHT,

But THE LIGHT is not diminished and it goes right on shining.

THE LIGHT knows that one way or another THE DARKNESS will once again Be THE LIGHT.

THE DARKNESS scratches and claws now with desperation at THE LIGHT

As THE LIGHT goes on shining.

In the distance THE LIGHT sparkles as it recognizes something in THE DARKNESS

And THE LIGHT goes right on shining.

THE DARKNESS is full of loathing not for THE LIGHT but for all of THE DARKNESS

And THE LIGHT goes on shining.

THE DARKNESS is beginning to remember that it was once also THE LIGHT

As THE LIGHT goes on shining it shimmers more beautifully than before.

THE DARKNESS recalls how it began, gradually at first then quickening the pace of darkness

As THE LIGHT beams brighter and keeps on shining.

THE DARKNESS begins to weep

There, there now THE LIGHT seems to say to THE DARKNESS,

And… in THE DARKNESS there comes a *flicker*…a small *glow*

And THE LIGHT sparks fully ablaze, dazzling, and positively luminous now in what was once THE DARKNESS.

Caring for Hummingbirds

*I*t takes a little diligence to provide hummingbirds with a healthy food source. I consider it a small price to pay to attract the feathered treasures to our home each year.

I am not a hummingbird expert, only someone passionately curious about them, so the following tips are only a guideline. Additional information on creating an environment conducive to hummingbirds may be found at various websites dedicated to these little marvels.

Make your own hummingbird feeder solution: 1 part table sugar dissolved in 4 parts water, boiled 1 to 2 minutes. Cool and store excess in the refrigerator. *Do not use artificial sweeteners, which may be harmful to hummers, or honey, which quickly spoils.*

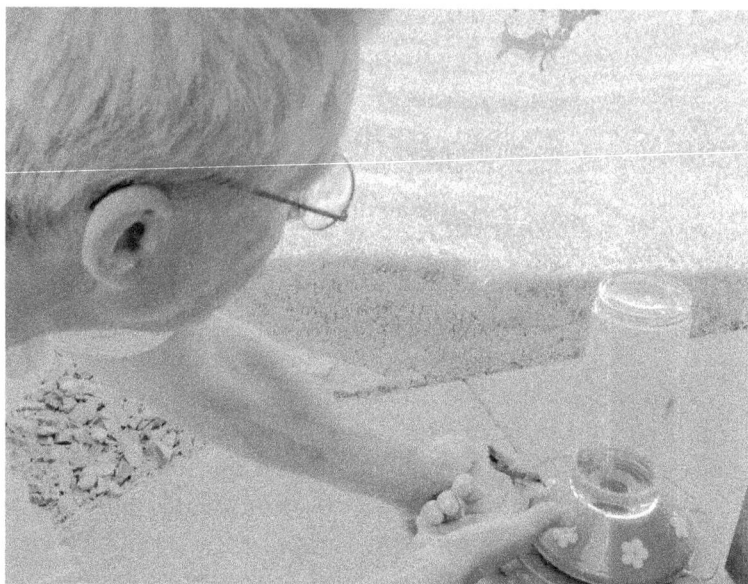

Never use dyes or food coloring in your feeder. Dye may be harmful to hummingbirds, and it will prevent you from properly monitoring the feeder solution for freshness.

Clean the feeders every two to three days, using a bottle brush to meticulously scour before rinsing, drying, and refilling.

Warm weather quickly fouls the hummingbird feeder solution. If you detect an odor or the liquid appears cloudy, remove the feeder at once and clean it thoroughly. Black spots are mold that must be removed immediately. Foul nectar can harm the birds.

Hang your feeders where the birds will have some protection from the elements, and a minimum of four to five feet off the ground to prevent predator access.

Hummingbirds love a shower to keep their tiny feathers free of sticky nectar. Outdoor sprinklers provide a quick cleanup on the go, and plenty of entertainment for you!

Be sure to hang your feeders at the first sign of hummingbird activity early in the season. Or, if you know when to expect them annually, go ahead and hang them up at that time, monitoring bird arrivals and cleaning feeders regularly as needed.

Depending upon the number of birds that use your feeder, you may find you only need to add a few ounces of liquid at a time. This is especially true in early season when birds are just arriving, and again when the weather is hot, as the nectar will have a tendency to spoil quickly in the heat; you will need to clean and refill feeders more often during hot weather, so refilling with a small amount each time will mean less waste.

Mild temperatures and high activity at your feeder may require that you clean and refill the bottles daily. *Wahoo!* That means many feathered friends are visiting your backyard oasis. *The more the merrier in my book!*

Go green! Reduce or eliminate the use of pesticides around your home. Hummers rely on small insects as a source of nutrients in their diet.

Go crazy with flowers and blooming shrubs! Hummers cannot resist the color red or bell-shaped flowers, which appear to grow just to entice them to help with the pollination process. Some flowers the hummers visit while in my yard include bright-colored petunias, million bells, lantana, bee balm, catmint, purple salvia, fuchsia, and Japanese lilac. This year I plan to add honeysuckle and columbine to the landscape for even more tantalizing dining options!

Have fun getting to know the flying jewels around your home!

Recommended Reading

I view my books as wise counselors, and friends. My philosophy is to take what I read, internalize the ideas that resonate with me, and adapt them to my own life applying the principles where I can.

Following are some of the books I appreciate for self-development:

Leadership/Management:

Energy Leadership, Transforming Your Workplace and Your Life from the Core by Bruce D Schneider

The 7 Habits of Highly Effective People by Steven R. Covey

The 8th Habit From Effectiveness to Greatness by Steven R. Covey

Leadership Gold by John C. Maxwell

The One Minute Manager by Kenneth Blanchard, Ph.D. and Spencer Johnson M.D.

Hey Leader ... Wake Up and Hear the Feedback by Eric Harvey

Personal Development:

The Success Principles, How to Get from Where You Are to Where You Want to Be by Jack Canfield

The Power of Intention by Dr. Wayne W. Dyer

Think and Grow Rich by Napoleon Hill

Life's Greatest Lessons, 20 Things That Matter by Hal Urban

Go Put Your Strengths to Work by Marcus Buckingham

Relationships:

Loving Each Other, The Challenge of Human Relationships by Leo F. Buscaglia

Born For Love, Reflections on Loving by Leo Buscaglia

Transition:

When Everything Changes, Change Everything by
    Neale Donald Walsch
Who Moved My Cheese? by Spencer Johnson M.D.

About the Author

S herri Gerek founded *Let's Strut Your Stuff* in 2010 to serve busy, ambitious women with individual coaching, motivational workshops, and seminars. Sherri leads an active life and loves to coach, write, travel, and cook from scratch. Her background includes 27 years of sales and marketing in the Travel and Hospitality Industry, training, leading and developing employees to reach their peak potential. In recent years, those roles included Departmental Manager for RSSC (Carlson Companies), World's Best Small Cruise Line according to *Conde` Nast Traveler* and *Travel and Leisure Magazine*. Sherri was opening and start-up Director of Sales

and Marketing for a Hilton Garden Inn Conference Center near her home.

As a certified professional coach, Sherri is passionate about helping others identify, and overcome the barriers to their highest aspirations. Sharing concepts on what it takes to achieve personal success, effective communication, and rewarding relationships, Sherri aims to inspire new solutions to old problems. The surest way to live a phenomenal life according to Sherri is to continually ask, and answer: *What is the highest vision I hold of myself, and what choice will I make right now to fully align with that vision?*

Sherri regularly blogs on her website: www.letsstrutyourstuff. com and she writes a monthly e-newsletter for her subscribers providing practical tips for living a full and happy life. Sherri's monthly column: *Ask the Coach—Let's Strut Your Stuff* appears in *Montana Woman Magazine.*

Sherri and her husband, Larry, live on Montana's Flathead River near Glacier National Park.

www.ingramcontent.com/pod-product-compliance
Lightning Source LLC
Chambersburg PA
CBHW072120020426
42334CB00018B/1655